Name of Title: Autoploidy, chromosomal differentiation and genetic affinity in _Oryza_ _sativa_ L.

Name of Author: Dr. Sharafat Hossain KHAN
2028 E Ben White Blvd 240-1729
Austin, TX 78741

Ex- Director,
Institute of Postgraduate Studies in Agriculture, Dhaka, Bangladesh

ABSTRACT

All chromosomes of rice have submedian centromeres except Chromosomes 4 which has a subterminal centromere. The three largest chromosomes showed two such constrictions, one on each arm. Haploid mitotic chromosomes showed the existence of four pairs of chromosomes with similar size and morphology. The largest four chromosomes could not be paired on this basis. Chromomere pattern at pachytene for all chromosomes were distinct. However, the chromomeric heterochromatin appeared frequently to resolve into smaller units. One or more euchromatic gaps of various sizes were observed for most chromosomes. These were terminal or interstitial and produced smaller nucleoli at various times in development. Up to four pairs of bivalents were found to have similar chromomeric patterns for corresponding to the mitotic findings. Chromosome 9 was found to be the nucleolar organizing chromosomes with a smaller nucleolar chromosome (Chromosome 10) to support it. It also showed a 'collar' configuration which could be explained by a reverse tandem duplication involving two chromosomes.

Pachytene in the haploids revealed complete pairing between most of the supposingly univalent chromosomes thus confirming the presence of the duplicate chromosomes. Maximum pairing at pachytene was four complete bivalents plus a quadrivalent comprising the four largest chromosomes. Further diploid pachytene analysis of Chromosomes 1 & 3 and 2 & 4 to have similar chromomeric patterns indicating that these two pairs of chromosomes were originally the same in size and structure. Karyotype analysis thus strongly indicates O. sativa L. to have an autotetraploid origin derived from a n=6 chromosome ancestor which has undergone further differentiation in its chromosome and a complete chromosomal diploidizing through strict regulation of pairing into bivalents. A karyotype idiogram and a chromomeric map have been prepared.

Keywords: Cytogenetics of rice, Chromosome studies in Oryza sativa, Autoploidy in Oryza sativa

INTRODUCTION

The genus _Oryza_ consists of about 20 valid species. Of these, _Oryza_ _sativa_ L and _Oryza_ _glaberrima_ steud are cultivated. _Oryza_ _sativa_ L. is the only species which grows in both temperate and tropical climates, the others being only tropical. The behavior of chromosomes and genetic segregation or breeding behavior of any organism is strongly correlated. Opinions differ regarding karyotype, chromosomal versus genetic differentiation as the cause of intersubspecies (synonyms, intersubspecies, _indica_ x _japonica_) crosses, genetic constitution of the different cultivar and wild species of rice and the origin of cultivated rice and its progenitors.

Studies of rice (_Oryza sativa_ L.) are handicapped by the small size of the chromosomes and the lack of a satisfactory technique for revealing the details of chromosomes structure. Few workers has analyzed the mitotic complement of rice nor have they yielded any appreciable advance toward the identification of the chromosomes.   Disagreement is considerable even as to the centromeric position of different chromosomes. Attempts were also made to analyze the complement at pachytene but success also only moderate. Identification of each chromosome by its morphological features continued to be problem. It is difficult to stain rice pachytene chromosomes so that the details are in critical contrast. The bright field light microscope does not accentuate the differences in chromosome segments and chromomeric value to the same value that phase does. Overstaining of chromosomes, however, is frequently a problem with phase contrast microscopy obliterating all the details. A technique has been developed to overcome such difficulties by combining critical staining with phase contrast microscopy.

MATERIALS AND METHODS

Analysis of the rice karyotype was divided into 1) mitotic and 2) meiotic studies corresponding mostly on metaphase and pachytene of the respective divisions.

1) Seven diploid japoinica varieties and three haploid plants were studied mitotically:

1. Calrose   (CI 8988)

2. Colusa (CI 1600)

3. CS-M3   (CI 9675)

4. ABB (IRRI Accession No. 99825.

5. I.V. 408 (Yukara x T(N) – 1)

6. Kulu   (PI 339730)

7. Italica Livorno   (PI 291478)

8. 72/7861 - a haploid plant derived from the cross Calady (ms) x Colusa/2

9. CS-M3-1 - haploid found in an F2 population of CS-M3(ms) x fertile CS-M3

10. CS-M3-2 - haploid found in the trisomic progeny

2) Pachytene studies were made on both indica and five japonica types and the three haploids:

1. CS-M3

2. Calrose

3. Kulu

4. 9052 - F4 selection of Caloro and Italica Livorno

5. T(N)-1 – (Taichung Native-1)

6. 72/7861   7. CS-M3 – 1   8. CS-M3 – 2 - Haploid, japonica type

Experimental methods

Phase contrast microscopy was utilized for all cytological studies. The following schedules were used for   a) mitotic studies and   b) phacytene preparation (Khan 1975).

RESULTS

1. Karyotype study (Mitosis)

A. Diploid mitosis

No variation in chromosome morphology was apparent at mitotic metaphase among the varieties studied. All but three small pairs of chromosomes showed one or more secondary constrictions at late prophase or prometaphase of mitosis (Fig 1a, b). However, only six pairs of chromosomes could be recognized as having a secondary constriction at metaphase. These six pairs of chromosomes comprise the 1st, 2nd, 3rd, 4th, 5th and 9th pairs designated according to their relative lengths on the metaphase plates. The biggest chromosome, hereinafter called Chromosome 1, has a submedian constriction, and is characterized by two more secondary constrictions, one on each arm. This chromosome occasionally shows two dark staining knobs, one on each arm, which could be satellites. Chromosome 2, the second largest in relative lengths, is also characterized by two constrictions, one on each arm. The centromere is barely submedian and can be misinterpreted as median. The centromere of the third chromosome is also submedian, with a prominent secondary constriction on the long arm. Chromosome 4 has a subterminal constriction and occasionally shows a secondary constriction on the long arm easily observed in the mitotic metaphase of haploids.

The 5th chromosome has a submedian centromere and it is also characterized by a constriction on the long arm. The 9th pair, on the other hand, has a prominent satellite on the short arm with a big nucleolar gap and it is always seen attached to the nucleolus at midprophase. The centric constriction is subterminal to submedian (including the satellite). All other chromosomes are submedian in centric position and do not present any other distinctive features at metaphase. Some of the chromosome pairs has nearly equal length. Figures 1a, b also show the presence of several pairs of small chromosomes having similar morphology and terminal satellites.

B. Haploid mitosis

Identification of the chromosomes in the diploid mitosis appeared difficult because of the presence of many smaller chromosomes having nearly the same size. The inherent variability produced by differential elongation of individual chromosomes during squashing also contributed to this problem. A good example of this is found in the quasi-tetraploid cells in which the separated daughter chromosomes are lying beside each other in the metaphase plate (no spindle is found in the dividing cells of pretreated roots so the daughter chromosomes separate and result in a tetraploid cell). Haploids are considered best for cytological interpretations in such cases since each chromosome is represented only once in the cells. The chromosomes of haploids permitted better identification. Figure 2b represents one typical haploid cells in mitotic metaphase. The centromere of each chromosome can be clearly determined. Except for chromosomes 4, 9 and 10, all others are submedian. Chromosomes 4 is very nearly subterminal. Chromosomes 9 and 10 show their terminal nucleolar organizer regions as distended euchromatic segments. Excluding the nucleolar organizer region, chromosome 9 appears subterminal whereas chromosomes 10 appears subterminal to submedian. Adding together their respective nucleolar organizer regions, they have the same total length. In more condensed cases, where the nucleolar organizers are also tightly coiled and are not apparent, both the chromosomes appear submedian. Chromosomes 7 and 8, though classified as submedian, are very nearly median. They also measure the same in most cases. Chromosome measurements were taken and arm ratios obtained for all the chromosomes from metaphase plates of similarly well-spread cells (Table 1). Some of the measurements were compared back with enlarged photographs of the same cell. As mentioned earlier, some chromosomes appeared and measured the same. In fact, in the haploid complement, some of the chromosomes could be classified as pairs (up to four pairs) based on their size, centromeric constrictions and other morphological features. The largest four chromosomes, however, cannot be paired based on these criteria.

2. Karyotype study (Meiosis)

A. Diploid pachytene

All the varieties were studied at pachytene, as this stage presents maximum structural details of the chromosomes. The chromomeric analysis at this stage showed details which were not presented in the mitotic chromosomes. No appreciable difference in the structure of the different chromosomes could be detected among the varieties studied. 'Kulu, an Australian introduction to this country (U.S.A) was distinctive in having only one bivalent attached to the nucleolus instead of the usual two. Further, 'Caloro' provided a much easier pachytene preparation than any of the other varieties. No detectable difference could be found in the only studied _indica_ variety T(N)-1 either although the chromomeres of this variety tended to stain deeper and were not spread out as in the _japonica_ varieties. As a result, some congregation of close chromomere appeared as heterochromatic blocks. Lighter staining, however, revealed the details in these regions. The nucleolus appeared 'budded' in most varieties with one smaller sphere fused to a larger one.

Two to five chromosomes could be seen attached to the nucleolus in a few cells instead of the usual two (Fig. 3a). Smaller nucleoli were produced by many of the other chromosomes and fusion of these nucleoli to the main nucleolus resulted in a multi-budded structure with more than two chromosomes attached to it. Although the chromomeric details could be studied easily, considerable difficulty was encountered in analyzing the chromosomes for their characteristic chromomeric patterns. One of the primary difficulties was the differential stretching of the chromosomes. The same chromosome would present notably different details depending on the stage of development and the amount of stretching resulting from squashing. The chromomeric heterochromatin in rice appear frequently to stretch out and resolve into smaller chromomeres (Fig. 3b) occasionally to the point of being completely euchromatic. The chromosomes, however, do retain their characteristic chromomeric patterns when squashed carefully (Figs. 4 and 5).

Centromere location at late pachytene was difficult to determine for a few chromosomes because of the presence of a few small euchromatic gaps which could be confused with the centromeres. In such cases, arm ratios obtained in mitotic studies for these chromosomes were used to generally locate the position of the centromere first. This was later confirmed from study of mid pachytene and lightly stained chromosomes. The centromeric chromomeres usually were apparent in such preparations.

<u>Descriptions of the chromosomes</u>

In the following pages, a description of each of the chromosomes of the complement is presented. The length of pachytene chromosomes were not measured because of the stretching artifact. Instead, a short summary of the relative lengths of individual chromosomes showing the mean and range in microns based on mitotic chromosomes of haploids is presented as a guide in Table 2.

1. The largest chromosome of the complement has a submedian centromeric constriction (Figs. 4, 5 and 1 in Fig. 11). Characteristic features of this chromosome, aside from its length include four distinct dark staining chromomeres at the distal end of the short arm. Occasionally, two distinct terminal satellites are seen, one on each arm. The centromere is flanked by a series of 10 to 12 distinct chromomeres on the short arm and two on the long arm. Two more prominent chromomeres could be seen midway of the long arm delimiting a gap. If in mid-pachytene, during squashing, this chromosome may become almost completely euchromatic except for the para-centromeric heterochromatin and the two centromeres mentioned above.

2. The second largest chromosome is submedian in centromeric constriction. At pachytene, its length is about equal to Chromosome 1. The centromere is flanked by four to five chromomeres on the long arm (Fig. 4, 5 and 2 in Fig. 11). A euchromatic gap follows these chromomeres. The short arm has six to seven large chromomeres flanking the centromere. A

rather large euchromatic gap follows two chromomeres next to the centromere on this arm. There are three to four moderate-sized chromomeres about the center or two-third of the long arm away from the centromere. A darkly stained satellite is present at the end of long arm. Four to five dark staining chromomeres (Fig. 5) can be seen occasionally at the terminal end of the short arm. In this figure, the long arm can also be seen attached to the nucleolus by a euchromatic segment following three to four large chromomeres at about two-thirds of its length.

3.   Centromere position of the 3rd chromosome is submedian. It is characterized by a rather prominent satellite on the short arm. The centromere is flanked by a group of chromomeres on either side (Fig. 4, 5 and 3 of Fig. 11). The centromeric chromomere is followed by four to five dark chromomeres on the short arm. A euchromatic gap is present on the long arm after two chromomeres flanking the centromere. This chromosome can occasionally be seen attached to the main nucleolus at this segment. Another dark staining chromomere also is visible after about three chromomeres away from this gap. A slightly less prominent satellite also can be seen at the end of the long arm. A prominent chromomere is present about midway of the long m which can be used as a marker.

4. This is the most distinctive and easily recognizable chromosome of the complement. The centromere appears to be subterminal (Fig. 4, 5 and 4 of Fig. 11). The short arm is almost completely heterochromatic due mainly to the presence of a series of large chromomeres. The centromere divides the heterochromatic short arm from the largely euchromatic long arm. The chromomeres in the short arm appear to be composed of mostly constitutive heterochromatin which seldom resolve into smaller units. The short arm has two chromomeres following the centromere which is followed by a large euchromatic gap (different in staining from other euchromatin). This gap would produce a small nucleolar body. Two more chromomeres after

this gap and there is another smaller gap which is also a nucleolar organizer region. The short arm ends with two more prominent chromomeres and a small satellite following this gap. The satellite region also produces an occasional small nucleolus (Fig. 6a). This nucleolar gap can be seen most easily at mid-pachytene. Except for a few moderate sized chromomeres immediately following the centromere, the long arm is almost featureless. A few faint but moderately large sized chromomeres also can be seen at about two-thirds of the long arm away from the centromere. At this position, though there is no characteristic gap pattern, this chromosome occasionally will attach itself to the nucleolus. A small nucleolar body is produced infrequently at this region when it is not attached to the principal nucleolus. A small satellite also is recognizable at the end of the long arm (Fig. 6 b). Its presence is confirmed further by an occasional nucleolus at the end.

5/6. These two chromosomes appear identical in good preparations (Fig. 4, 5 and 5/6 of Fig. 11). Both have submedian centromeres and a terminal deeply staining satellite on the long arm. Only one of them produces a small nucleolus at this constriction point at any one time but whether the same chromosome is involved each time is difficult to ascertain without other markers. In normal preparations, the chromosomes may look somewhat different except for the terminal satellites and the centromere. The centromeric chromomeres appear unequal, the larger one being on the short arm. A euchromatic gap follows the centromere on the long arm which is again followed by seven moderate-sized chromomeres. Another group of about four chromomeres following these is isolated by a gap on either side. There is one more distinct chromomere following this last gap. In fact, these last two chromomeres delimiting this gap show up as markers when other chromomeres may have resolved into smaller units. These two chromomeres can be located at about three-fourths the length of the long arm away from the centromere. The short arm has three medium-sized chromomeres immediately following the centromere. One of these two chromosomes can be seen attached to the nucleolus by its satellite occasionally.

7 /8. These two chromosomes appear identical in carefully prepared slides. Both are submedian in centric constrictions. But they can be interpreted as median since they have a very high arm ratio (0.92%). Both have a euchromatic gap immediately following the centromere on the short arm. There is a series of four large chromomeres following this gap, then a smaller gap. Four to five more chromomeres and the short arm ends with a rather prominent satellite (Fig. 4, 5 and 7//8 of Fig.11) The long arm has six to seven chromomeres following the centromere. The centromere is very small delimited by two equal sized chromomeres. These two centromeric chromomeres are also the largest ones for these two chromosomes.

9/10. These two chromosomes are again very similar in their morphology (Fig. 4, 5 and 9/10 of Fig. 11). Both are prominently satellited, both show the same general features but there are some variations in certain finer detail. Chromosome 9 has the nucleolar organizer for the principal nucleolus. This was evident from pachytene analysis of the Australian variety, "Kulu" in which only this chromosome was found attached to the main nucleolus. The size and variability of the nucleolus apparently was not affected by the non-attachment of Chromosome 10. At pachytene in haploids, Chromosome 9 shows a much longer nucleolar organizer region. The centromeres of these two chromosomes appear subterminal to submedian at pachytene, whereas at mitosis, they appear submedian. Both chromosomes remain attached to the junction of the compound (budded) nucleolus. It is difficult to observe the exact difference between the two chromosomes at this point. The short arm of Chromosome 10 has five rather large chromomeres including the satellite whereas Chromosome 9 has seven small to medium sized chromomeres in the same arm. One of the most interesting observations on the difference between these two chromosomes is the frequent formation of a 'collar' type configuration on the short arm of Chromosome 9 (Fig. 7 a, b). The 'collar' involves at least four small chromosomes. Both <u>indica</u> and <u>japonica</u> varieties show this configuration on this chromosome. The nucleolus appears budded with one large and one small unit partially fused together. In some preparations, this appearance clearly is due to the production of one nucleolus by each of the homologues of Chromosome 9. Thus, it is actually a compound nucleolus. The size of the nucleolus produced by each of the homologues varies depending on the variety and stage of development. Some varieties show only one nucleolus most of the time whereas others showing mostly compound nucleolus may produce a single nucleolus in a few cells. The long arms of Chromosome 9 and 10 show a series of five medium to large sized chromosomes. A smaller gap may be evident after the first three chromomere following the centromere in the long arm. Both chromosomes show a terminal dark staining chromomeres which is most likely a small satellite as occasionally a small nucleolar body is produced by one of these chromosomes at this site.   Another somewhat distinct chromomeres can be seen just prior to the satellite.

11/12. This pair of chromosomes is very characteristic in that it is very easy to recognize at pachytene (Fig. 4 and 11/12 of Fig. 11). Like Chromosome 4, the heterochromatin in these two chromosomes rarely resolves into smaller units. The centromere is submedian and the chromosomes are characterized by a large euchromatic gap in the middle of the chromosomes. This is the largest gap in any of the chromosomes of the complement and stains slightly different from other euchromatin. A small nucleolus is produced occasionally at this gap, most probably by only one of the pair. Many times, one of these two chromosomes can be seen attached to the main nucleolus with or without the production of a smaller nucleolus at this gap. The euchromatic gap is flanked by four large chromomeres on one side and three on the other, the last two of which enclose the centromere. A small gap follows the centromere on the short arm with eight to nine medium sized chromomeres interspersed thought out. A faint satellite chromomeres occasionally may be seen at the end of this arm. The long arm has about three more chromomeres immediately following the four dark chromomeres flanking the euchromatic gap. There is a smaller gap between these two groups of chromomeres.

B. Haploid pachytene

In view of the structural similarities observed between pairs of bivalents at the diploid level, it was felt necessary to study the pachytene of haploids. Pachytene in all the haploids studied showed complete pairing between the chromosomes. Maximum pairing observed was four complete bivalents plus a quadrivalent involving the four largest chromosomes (Fig. 9 a, b). The fourth chromosome, which is the most distinctive in the diploid because of the heterochromatic short arm, pairs completely with a larger chromosomes except for the terminal two to three chromomeres. This larger chromosome again pairs with another for the rest of its length. It is apparent then that Chromosome 4 was involved in a translocation with another chromosome. This then accounts for a fifth pair. The other two chromosomes were mostly unpaired while one of them has a great deal of fold back pairing. Previous information on the chromomeric pattern of these four chromosomes indicates that both chromosomes 1 and 2 have similar distal ends (both show four dark staining chromomeres of the short arm (Fig. 5). Chromosome 2 also have a prominent gap following the centromere as in Chromosome 4 and continues with a six to seven moderately large chromosomes on the short arm. Chromosomes 1 and 3 also show a series of chromomeres comparable to each other in number and position except that Chromosome 1 has a longer arm with a terminal end similar to Chromosome 2. Reconstituting the chromosome according to the above information, it is evident that Chromosomes 2 and 4 were identical prior to translocation and so were Chromosome 1 and 3. Chromosome 1 become the longest of the complement as a result of unequal translocation with one of the partners of Chromosome 2, now a much shorter Chromosome 4. Further evidence is obtained from length measurement of these chromosomes in the haploid complement (Table 1).

The difference between the lengths of Chromosome 1 and 3 is approximately equal to that between Chromosomes 2 and 4 in some cells, The secondary constriction patterns for these two pairs of chromosomes also conform to their respective partners. From the results thus obtained on chromosome structure at mitosis and meiosis of both the diploid and haploid materials, a revised karyotype of rice is presented in idiogram Figure 10 and a chromomeric map of all twelve chromosomes in Figure 11.

DISCUSSIONS

Chromosome Morphology and Identification of Chromosomes

Several characteristics usually are considered in identifying or characterizing any or particular chromosome. These are (1) chromosome length (2) centromeric position or arm ratio (3) presence or absence of satellites and their position and size (4) presence or absence of heterochromatic segments and their location and (5) presence or absence of other secondary consideration.

A. Structural features of Chromosome 1.

As was mentioned earlier, there is considerable disagreement regarding the exact centromeric position on the different chromosomes (Table 3). Most workers agree that the largest chromosome, Chromosome 1, make up for about 12 to 13% of the total chromatin. Shastry et al. (1960), however, found it to be 20%. Such discrepancies between the results of these authors and other researchers were attributed to the differences in the material used for cytological studies (Shastry, 1964). No additional features were described for the chromosome by earlier researchers studying the mitotic chromosome. The present investigation, however, showed that two constrictions occasionally are seen, one on each arm, in this chromosome (Fig. 3). At pachytene, sharply defined chromosomes were visible at both ends of the chromosome (Shastry et al., 1960) with uniform staining in other regions. The present study revealed four distinct terminal chromomeres in the short arm only. Shastry and coworkers were unable to analyze the heteropynotic areas flanking the centromere which contains about ten chromomeres on the short arm and two on the long arm. This chromosome is also distinguished by two small satellites, one on either end, which are only occasionally visible.

B. Structural features of Chromosomes 2

The second chromosome is distinctive with prominent secondary constriction, one on each arm, at mitosis. Two previous workers (Hu, 1958; Ishii and Mitsukuri, 1960) noted a secondary constriction on the long arm of this chromosome but failed to observe one in the short arm. There is some disagreement as to the centromeric classification of this chromosome. The centromere, being located close to the centre, has occasionally being interpreted as median, but it is actually submedian with an arm ratio of 0.88. At pachytene, this chromosome has been classified submedian by Shastry et. al.(1960) with distinct chromomeres on both arms and sharply defined chromomeres adjacent to the centromeric heterochromatin of the long arm. Again, a very clear chromomeric pattern was observable for the para-centromeric heterochromatin. A small satellite is frequently seen at the end of long arm. The most notable characteristic for this chromosome, however, is a distinct euchromatic gap at mid-length. There are four to five terminals deeply stained chromomeres on the short arm, similar to those on the short arm of Chromosome 1. The evolutionary significance of this similarity will be discussed later.

C. Structural features of Chromosome 3

Chromosome 3 is submedian in agreement with most of the rice researchers. However, Shastry et al (1960) thought it to be almost median. No other descriptive features were reported by other workers for this chromosome at mitosis. The present study revealed a prominent gap in the long arm. This gap corresponds quite well with the euchromatic gap found by this author at pachytene in this chromosome. The chromomeric pattern of this chromosome also is quite comparable to that of Chromosome 1 except for the length of the short arm. Chromosome 1 has a longer short arm with a different terminal end. The secondary constrictions found in the long arm of both these chromosomes at mitosis, however, seem to correspond. At pachytene, however, no comparable euchromatic gap was observable in the long arm of Chromosome 1. A rather prominent satellite is frequently seen at the end of the short arm of Chromosome 3. Another fainter satellite is sometimes visible on the long arm with an occasional small body attached to it.

D. Structural feature of Chromosome 4

Considerable disagreement exists regarding the centromeric position on Chromosome 4. The present investigation clearly shows it to be subterminal. No secondary constrictions have been reported for this chromosome though at mitosis of haploid, the present author observed an occasional gap in the long arm. At pachytene, this chromosome was classified as submedian by Shastry et al. (1960), with an intensely stained terminal region in which the chromomeric details were indistinct. They identified the short arm by a longer heterochromatic terminal region and distinct proximal chromomeres. Their description, however, does not quite conform to the results obtained in the present study. This is the most distinctive chromosome of the complement, having a concentration of large chromomere of the short arm only. It is also characterized by two small satellites, one on either end (Fig. 6 a, b). Small nucleolar bodies are produced sporadically by these satellites. In addition, there are two other sites, one, the euchromatic gap on the short arm and the other, at about two-thirds of the length of the long arm away from the centromere, which produce small nucleolar bodies at certain times.

<u>Duplicate Chromosomes and the Problem of Identification of Individual Chromosomes</u>

At this point, it seems appropriate to discuss a few other problems relating to the chromosome morphology and identification of individual chromosomes of rice. Nandi (1936), based on his studies on mitosis and association of bivalents at meiotic metaphase, assumed that the basic chromosome number of rice, <u>O</u>. <u>sativa</u> L., was <u>n</u>=5. The present-day rice with <u>n</u>=12 presumably was derived secondarily by doubling of a cross between two 5-chromosome species. A duplication of one chromosome in each contributing genome prior to hybridization, was postulated to achieve this (a detailed discussion on this follows somewhat later). However, none of the research workers involved either in mitotic or meiotic studies could detect the presence of any duplicate chromosomes. In the present investigation, the author, however, noted strong similarities between three or four pairs of bivalents. This was confirmed by later studies of haploid pachytene where the similar chromosomes paired completely with perfect chromomere by chromomere matching. One probable reason for this failure of other workers to detect similarities between bivalents is the nature of the heterochromatin of rice. Although the chromomeric heterochromatin presence a characteristic pattern, it frequently resolves into smaller chromomeres under pressure during squashing. Another fact which has become apparent from the present investigation is the differential stretching of individual chromosomes in relation to each other. Chromosomes of the same size or of closely similar sizes may thus alter their relative size relationships. Variation in arm ratio due to differential stretching in the two arms of the same chromosome may occur. These facts became apparent once it was recognized that there were morphologically and structurally similar chromosomes in some cells which were dissimilar in others. Staining difficulties were probably one of the main problems limiting other workers in making exact interpretations.

E. Structural features of Chromosomes 5 and 6

Chromosome 5 is considered submedian by all workers. No other distinctive features were reported at mitosis. A secondary constriction on the long arm, however, was found by this author. Shastry <u>et al.</u> (1960) described this chromosome as having darkly stained terminal regions. In the middle of the long arm, there was another darkly stained region 3 to 4 micron long. The description of Chromosome 6 needs also to be considered here in view of the duplicate nature of these two chromosomes. Chromosome 6 is considered subtelocentric at meiosis (Shastry <u>et al.</u>, 1960) and submedian at mitosis by many. Terminal and subterminal regions of both arms reportedly have darkly stained segments (Shastry et al., 1960). No mitotic chromosome in the haploid <u>O.</u> <u>sativa</u> complement was found to have a subtelocentric constriction. The nucleolar organizer chromosome at mitosis sometimes gives an arm ratio of 0.33 excluding the nucleolar organizer region. At pachytene, however, the nucleolar chromosomes appear subterminal with an arm ratio of 0.25. But in cells where the chromosomes have retained much of their chromomeric patterns and relative size relationships, these two chromosomes show an arm ratio of 0.33 which is in agreement with the findings in haploid mitosis. The probability that a different chromosome was described which may or may not have stretched to the same degree as the other chromosomes is also high in view of the evidence for such occurrences in the present study. Inadequate descriptions and lack of photographs in Shastry and co-workers report make it difficult to identify these chromosomes for comparative study. One other probability is that they could be the nucleolar chromosomes of the present study since they correspond roughly to the descriptions given by Shastry <u>et al.</u> (1960). However, there is no information as to whether or not any of these chromosomes were found attached to the main nucleolus at any time.

F. Structural features of Chromosomes 7 and 8

Chromosomes 7 and 8 also form a bivalent in haploid pachytene and as such will be discussed together. Reports on mitotic studies are again contradictory regarding the centromeric position. Hu (1964) considers number 8 as the nucleolar organizer chromosome. In the present study, both are found to be submedian with an arm ratio of 0.92. At pachytene, Chromosome 7 was described a median with one arm darker than the other and with an intensively terminal segment about 4 microns long. Chromosome 8, on the other hand, was considered submedian, the long arm of which has three distinct chromomeres while the short arm has six distinct chromomeres in the terminal region (Shastry <u>et al.</u>,1960). However, results obtained by the present author differ considerably. Regarding Chromosome 7, there are only three chromosomes in the complement which can be seen to have darkly stained terminal regions and are also somewhat comparable in length measurements. These are numbers 4, 9 and 10, all of which are clearly submedian or subterminal in centric constructions. Their chromomeric patterns are distinctive and differs from Shastry's descriptions.

G. Structural features of Chromosomes 9 and 10

Chromosomes 9 and 10 are almost always found attached to the nucleolus. Characterized by submedian to subterminal constrictions and a prominent satellite on the short arm, they also are a pair of duplicate chromosomes. While most reports on mitotic chromosomes agree with the submedian classification of Chromosome 9, disagreement prevails regarding the same in Chromosome 10.

i) Nucleolar organizer regions of Chromosomes 9 and 10

Diploid metaphases vary rarely showed a second pair of chromosomes with a nucleolar gap or satellited region at mitosis but in the haploids, frequently two chromosomes would be seen with satellites corresponding to the two nucleolar chromosomes. Slight differences can be observed in the short arms of these two chromosomes (Fig. 2 b). The sectors of dark staining chromatin in the short arm of Chromosome 9 is slightly less than that of Chromosome 10 but the length of the distended nucleolar organizer region of Chromosome 9 in longer than in Chromosome 10. The reason for this discrepancy can be found in the pachytene of the diploids and haploids. Shastry et al. (1960) described Chromosome 9 as submedian with five to six distinct large chromomeres on the short arm, Chromosome 10 is, however, considered subtelocentric with a very small short arm and intensely staining region about three microns long on the long arm. These descriptions fit those for Chromosome 10 and 9 respectively fairly well but the present study revealed a few additional interesting details. Chromosome 10 was found to have five large chromomeres on the short arm following the centromere and ending in a rather large satellite with a negligible nucleolar gap. The short arm of chromosome 9, on the other hand, shows a series of seven medium to small chromomeres for the same region, ending in a large satellite but having a much longer nucleolar organizer region between these two chromosomes could have resulted from a deletion in this segment in chromosome 10. Figure 8 shows these two chromosomes paired in the haploid pachytene and illustrates the difference in the lengths of this region. But whether the deletion occurred prior to doubling or post-doubling of chromosomes has not been determined yet.

ii) 'Collar' configuration on the short arm of Chromosome 9

Regarding the difference in the number and size of chromomeres and the occurrence of the 'collar' chromosome on in the short arm of Chromosome 9 (Fig. 7a, b), it seems most likely that these two chromosomes may have evolved different degrees of coiling for the short arm resulting in larger chromomeres in chromosome 10. It may also be due to a probable inactivation of some of the genes in this segment of chromosome 10 by heterochromatization. The 'collar' configuration and the difference in number of chromomeres can be explained by assuming a reverse tandem duplication for a length of chromosome involving two chromomeres. Thus a 5-chromere segment would become a 7-chromere region. The 'collar' may form whenever pairing is initiated away from this particular segment so that pairing forces can act on this segment during the time it takes the zipper-fashion pairing to reach this point. Regular pairing may be observed without the 'collar' configuration because there was not time enough for pairing in this duplicated segment to occur if the initiation point was close. Diagrammatically, this can be illustrated in Fig. 12.

H. Structural features of Chromosomes 11 and 12

Chromosome 11 and 12 are considered submedian or median by different workers. Mitotic studies by this author confirmed them to be submedian with an arm ratio of 0.70. Pachytene descriptions of these two chromosomes given by Shastry et al. (1960) differ considerably from the results of the present investigation, although centromeric classification is the same. The short arm of Chromosome 11 was considered to be the darkest of the complement with a terminal knob. A gradient in size and stainability of chromomeres from distal to proximal region of the short arm was also noted by these authors. But results obtained by the present author clearly show that there is no chromosome in the complement with a gradient. However, because of the knob on the short arm, it is possible these chromosomes could be one of a pair comprised of Chromosome 7 and 8, which is characterized by a rather large dark staining satellite. Chromosome 12 is the smallest with two distinct chromomeres in the middle of the long arm (Shastry et al., 1960). According to the results obtained in the present study, Chromosome 11 and 12 are very distinctive and can be recognized as easily as Chromosome 4 by their euchromatic median gap flanked by large chromomeres. Unlike most other chromosomes, the heterochromatin of these two chromosomes persists through most of pachytene stage, withstanding the rigor of squashing.

CONCLUSIONS

Several interesting points become apparent from the above discussion. One is that extreme care must be used in preparing rice chromosomes for pachytene studies and those cells showing least distortion of the chromosomes should be used for identification and karyotype study. A second and intriguing point is the preponderance of chromosomes with the ability to organize smaller nucleoli. Most species are characterized by a pair or two (rarely more) satellited chromosomes. But in the present study, it has been observed that almost all the chromosomes produce one or more smaller nucleoli, at some time or other during development, the main nucleolus being produced by one of them. The nucleolar organizers may be terminal or interstitial, one or more per chromosome, and are variable in size. In reviewing the reports of the various workers, it also became apparent that many of their chromosomes could be paired according to their size and centromeric classification. Regarding the nucleolar organizer chromosomes, the different workers came up with different results. The nucleolar organizer chromosome has been described as No.3 by Shastry et al. (1960), No. 8 by Hu (1964), No. 10 by Wu (unpublished), and No. 4 by Ishii and Mitsukuri (1960), The present study showed clearly that Chromosome 9 is the nucleolar organizer along with Chromosome 10 based on information obtained from haploid mitosis and pachytene and also analyses of the various diploid. One variety, 'Kulu' has only Chromosome 9 as the nucleolar chromosome with no apparent change in the nucleolus when compared to those with both Chromosome 9 and 10. The reason for this contrary reports lies in the preponderances of chromosomes with smaller nucleolar organizers. Most of these chromosomes can be observed attached to the main nucleolus at some time or other during development, with or without the production of a separate nucleolus.

A. Origin of cultivated rice

Diploid wild species and the putative ancestor of rice.

The biological origin of rice is not certain. In one opinion, rice is presumed to have originated from a diploid ancestor with $\underline{n}$=12. Considerable disagreement, however, exists as to the identity of the putative ancestor. Three major hypotheses have been presented.

1) That cultivated rice has originated from <u>O.</u> <u>sativa</u> f. <u>spontanea</u>. Morphological differences are negligible between <u>sativa </u>and <u>spontanea</u> and they hybridize freely with each other forming fully fertile F1 hybrids (Oka, 1956b; Porteres, 1956; Richharia, 1960).

2) That it has originated from <u>Oryza</u> <u>perennis.</u> It is a perennial grass with three geographical sub-species, barthii; cubensis and <u>balunga</u>. These are different from each other in many characters. In genetic literatures, <u>O.</u> perennis occasionally included <u>O.</u> <u>sativa</u> f. <u>spontanea</u> (Oka and Chang. 1960; Morishima <u>et</u> <u>al.,</u> 1961). Incidentally, Asian <u>O.</u> <u>perennis </u>and <u>O.</u> <u>sativa</u> f. <u>spontanea </u>are easily hybridized with normal chromosome pairing and varying degrees of fertility in the F1s. Thus, both seem close to <u>sativa</u> and both may be progenitors of the cultivated form (Ramiah and Ghose, 1951; Sampath and Rau, 1951).

3) That <u>Oryza</u> <u>sativa</u> has originated from O. officinalis (Roschevicz, 1931; Chatterjee, 1951). This species also shows varying degrees of similarities in its morphological features to <u>Oryza</u> <u>sativa</u> L., Shastry <u>et</u> <u>al.</u> (1961) found nearly complete pairing in <u>sativa</u> x <u>officinalis</u> hybrids. However, most rice researchers (Sampath and Rau, 1951; Richharia, 1960; Yeh and Henderson, 1961a; Oka and Chang, 1962; Sampath, 1962 seem to agree on the Asian forms of Oryza perennis (<u>balunga </u>sub-species) as the probable progenitor of cultivated rice (Oryza <u>sativa</u>).

B. Secondary association and origin of rice

A second approach considers the origin of rice from the standpoint of secondary association of bivalents at metaphase-I. Secondary association of bivalents at metaphase-I has used as evidence for evolution through polyploidy and is interpreted as occurring between genetically and structurally equivalent chromosomes (in essentially the same fashion as in synapsis) due to a residual attraction (Lawrence, 1931; Darlington, 1937).   On the assumption that secondary association of bivalents do represent chromosomal ancestry, one can postulate that the number of groups at maximum association would give a clue to the original chromosomal of the ancestor or the progenitor. This has led many rice researchers to analyze the species from this standpoint. Most of them (Nandi, 1936; Sakai, 1935; Okuno, 1944; Hu, 1962; Parthasarathy, 1938) reported finding a maximum association forming five groups (2 groups of 3IIs and three groups of 2IIs) at metaphase-I. This, together with the findings of many duplicate genes (runners vs non-runners – Ramirez et el., 1960; duplicate fertility genes, gamete development genes – (Oka, 1953, 1956) led to the hypothesis that $\underline{O}$. $\underline{sativa}$ probably originated through hybridization between two 5-chromosome species which had one chromosome previously duplicated in each.   This event was followed by doubling of the entire set.   Thus, according to this hypothesis, cultivated rice is an allotetraploid derived from a basic number of $\underline{n}$=5, the present-day $\underline{n}$=12 being secondarily derived through aneuploidy and doubling.   However, Khan and Choudhury (unpublished data) found a maximum association of two groups of 6IIs each. The difficulty is assigning one ancestral chromosome for each group is apparent because in this case, the basic chromosome number becomes $\underline{n}$=2 and the transition from $\underline{n}$=2 to $\underline{n}$=12 is a rather difficult hypothesis to cope with. The possibility that the observation of two groups of 6IIs was a chance occurrence was nullified by the finding of similar associations in Prophase II chromosomes. Nearly 40% of the cells observed in that stage had two groups of 6Is.   In this regard, it may be mentioned that Morinaga and his co-workers (Morinaga and Fukushima, 1934; Morinaga, 1964) found a predominant segregation of six by six in the first anaphase of haploid meiosis, but they did not provide any explanation for this phenomenon. Further, in wide interspecific crosses which have been doubled to obtain fertility, the two contributing genomes maintain a separate identity as a group for many generations. These observations, together with this author's earlier findings led him to propose a new hypothesis regarding the origin of rice and the significance of secondary association of chromosomes.

The hypothesis runs thus:

That secondary association may be a manifestation of ancestral affinity for the chromosomes derived from a particular genome expressing itself whenever there is a chance to do so (as in the case of maintaining separate identity of genomes in wide interspecific crosses) and that the chromosomes may associate or group together purely as a matter of chance so that any two , three, four, five or six or all may come together in association depending on the relative position of each chromosome or bivalent at pachytene. Intervening chromosomes of the other genome may prevent larger associations. Since it assumes a sort of affinity and physical approximation, this may well be the reason why such secondary associations are mostly seen in plants with small chromosomes. Further, it is evident that the relative frequencies of groups of six, five, four, three, two and one would be minimum for the extremes, the maximum frequency being for groups of two and three or both together. This explains Morinag's findings and also those of Khan and Choudhury if it is assumed that two highly differentiated species, each with n=6, hybridized and then was naturally doubled to obtain fertility in the first amphidiploid. The origin of rice could be presented as shown in Fig. 13.

C. Haploid pairing and the origin of rice

Pachytene studies of the haploids contributed most significantly toward identification of the chromosomes and to a better understanding of the origin of cultivated rice, Oryza sativa L. Pairing at pachytene was extensive in the haploids with frequent formation of four complete bivalents and a multivalent, the exact nature of which was very difficult to ascertain at first. In one cell, however, a clear quadrivalent was seen involving the four largest chromosomes along with four complete bivalents. Chromosome 4 was completely paired with another chromosome except for a very short terminal segment on the short arm. Later studies revealed the other chromosome to be Chromosome 2. This chromosome also has a short arm characterized by four distinct terminal chromomeres, similar to those of the short arm of Chromosome 1. Chromosome 1, in turn, has a high degree of similarity in the chromomeric pattern of the long arm with that of Chromosomes 3. The short arm of Chromosomes 3 differs from that of

Chromosome 1 in that the number of chromomeres following the centromere is fewer and it is considerably shorter. At mitosis, Chromosome 3 also shows a secondary constriction on the long arm comparable to that of Chromosome 1. Both Chromosomes 2 and 4 occasionally attach themselves to the nucleolus at a comparable site on the long arm. The long arms of both these chromosomes are characterized by the presence of a small satellite in each. Also, there is a prominent euchromatic gap near the centromere (after two chromomeres in the short arm) on both Chromosome 2 and 4 and their chromomeric patterns are quite similar at diploid pachytene. Although generally not apparent, the short arm of Chromosome 2 may have a small satellite or nucleolar organizer at the end as occasionally a small nucleolus can be seen attached at that point. Chromosome 3 has a rather prominent satellite in the short arm which is replaced by a fainter one in Chromosome 1. Chromosome 4, on the other hand, has a satellite in the short arm comparable to that of Chromosome 3. All these observations point to the fact that Chromosomes 2 and 4 were originally the same and so were Chromosomes 1 and 3. As a result of an unequal reciprocal translocation between the short arms of 1 and 4, the same as number 3 and 2 respectively, Chromosome 1 became the longest chromosome of the complement while Chromosome 4 assumed the fourth position, giving four morphologically different chromosomes. Diagrammatically, the situation can be presented as shown in Fig. 14.

Evidence obtained thus far clearly indicate that 12 chromosomes of cultivated rice have originated for a base $\underline{n}$ = 6 by direct duplication of the set. Whether or not the chromosomal structural changes found in this study occurred pre-or post-duplication is yet to be determined – depending on the successful identification of the wild progenitor. Based on the cytological evidence presented here, it is quite evident that the basic chromosome number of cultivated rice is n-6, not n=5 as earlier assumed by most workers. The finding of pairing in the haploids does not necessarily invalidate the hypothesis proposed by this author on secondary association of bivalents. Instead, it confirms this author's earlier hypothesis of n=6 as the basic number proposed initially from observations on secondary association only. Whereas, in the earlier hypothesis, it was assumed that the contributing genomes were different, haploid pairing shows that the two genomes were originally the same. As earlier discussed, the genetic or chromosomal differentiation in the doubled genome could have occurred pre- or post – duplication. It is thus possible to envisage the origin of rice in the same line as proposed earlier assuming two highly differentiated lines or subspecies instead of two different species.

i) *Non-homologous pairing of chromosome in the haploid*

A few reports of non-homologous pairing occurring in monoploid or haploid individuals in the absence of homologous partners are available (McClintock, 1933 Sadasivaiah and Kasha, 1973). In view of such reports, the possibility of such pairing occurring in rice haploids needs to be examined. The degree and the nature of such pairing, however, varies in these reports and a generally acceptable explanation of such phenomenon is not available. Non-homologous pairing is usually explained as due to either heterochromatic fusion (Riley and Chapman, 1957) due to torsional effects extending from homologously to non-homologously paired regions (Darlington, 1937). Heterochromatic fusion is assumed to occur in a random fashion so no definite association pattern can be excepted in such cases. In Barely (Hordeum spp.- assumed to be basically a diploid), however, Sadasiviaiah and Kasha (1971) reported extensive pairing in haploids derived from interspecific crosses. Certain segments reportedly associate consistently. No information on the presence or detection of chromosomes with similar chromomeric pattern is available. In rice, however, similar chromosomes at mitosis do show similar chromomeric patterns (Fig. 4). Other chromosomes, even if of similar lengths, show a very different chromomeric patterns.

ii) *Cytological behavior of diploid and induced autoteraploids of rice*

a) Zygomere differentiation and preferential pairing

The completely diploid behavior of cultivated rice and cytological behavior of chromosomes in autotetraploids thereof, are open to criticism. In the author's opinion, the chromosomes of <u>O. sativa</u> L., during the process of evolution, have differentiated sufficiently genetically to warrant preferential pairing. According to Sybenga (1973), rearrangements and other structural differentiations aid in preferential pairing (Devine, 1967, Doyle, 1973; Stebbins, 1965; Sybenga, 1966, 1972a, b, 1973) among the four homologues of an autotetraploid but it is most effective when combined with zygomere differentiation (Zygomere = a hypothetical chromosomal unit of function specially involved in the achievement and regulation of pairing at meiotic prophase – proposed by Sybenga, 1966). Mutation in some zygomeres may alter their specificity. Thus, identical 'alleles' or zygomeres still attract each other effectively while different 'alleles' have recognition problem. In a slightly different situation, zygomeres may still have the specificity, but in one chromosomal genotype, some of them may have reduced activity or no activity at all. In another genotype, a different set or number of zygomeres may have altered thusly. The combined effect would be pairing only between chromosomal genotypes of identical zygomere specificity or on other words, preferential pairing without any appreciable structural changes.

b)   5B system of wheat in relation to pairing in rice

A genetic mechanism regulating pairing, similar to that of wheat (Sears and Okamoto, 1959; Riley and Chapman, 1958) could also be operative in rice. _Oryza_ _minuta_ which has a genome designation of CCDD may actually have the sativa (AA) genome it. There are several reports of good pairing in sativa x minuta hybrids. In an induced octoploid of <u>O</u>. <u>minuta</u> (2x=96, CC CCDDDD) which has all chromosomes present four times and can be considered a raw polyploid, the average frequency of tetravalents per pollen mother cell was found to be only 7.26 out of an expected 24 (Watanabe and Ono, 1966). But the most interesting observation pertinent to this discussion was that of a polyhaploid (x=48) cell. This cell, instead of showing 24IIs as in normal tetraploid <u>O</u>. <u>minuta</u> (2x=48), formed 6IV and 12IIs. Without delving into the mechanics of the actual origin of this cell, a situation analogous to the 5B chromosome system of wheat, can be visualized if this cell somehow lost the chromosome or chromosomes carrying such a gene or gene system or else did not respond to the homologous pairing suppressor.   Developing a set of nullisomics on <u>O</u>. <u>sativa</u> L., if possible, is thus desirable to clarify the problem.

D. Monosomics and nullisomics in rice

An indication of the autoploid nature of rice would be the occurrence of viable monosomics for most of its chromosomes, if not all. In fact, though none has so far attempted to establish a complete monosomic set, several reports of spontaneous occurrence of monosomics are available in rice (Chandrasekharan, 1952; Seshu and Venkataswamy, 1958; Sampath and Krisnaswamy, 1948). One of these (Sampath and Krisnaswamy, 1948) reported on a strain of rice which segregated for sterile tillers in a 1:2;1 ratio. The sterile were found to have 22 chromosomes (nullisomic). They concluded from their results that the strain was a 23-chromosome plant from which a 1:2:1 ratio was obtained for 24-;23-:22-chromosome types. Apparently the monosomics was not only viable but was fertile too.

E. Tetrasomic inheritance and autoploidy of rice

Another criticism can be made against any autoploid origin of rice is that no tetrasomic inheritance pattern for any character is known in <u>O</u>. <u>sativa.</u> A case in point is that of Alfalfa (Medicago spp.). only disomic inheritance patterns were obtained in earlier studies. However, Atwood and Grun (1951) pointed out that most of these studies were not extensive enough to distinguish between disomic and tetrasomic inheritance. It remained for Stanford (1951) to establish conclusively that the segregation was tetrasomic when he conducted a study of purple vs white flower color inheritance to the F3 generation.

ACKNOWLEDGEMENTS

The author's sincerest and deepest appreciation goes to Dr. J.N. Rutger for providing stimulating guidance throughout the course of the present investigation and extending financial assistance whenever needed. The author is also greatly indebted to Professor Charles M. Rick and Dr. Earlene A. Rupert for their constructive criticism of the manuscript and encouragements during difficult times. Special thanks also are due to Professor M.L. Paterson who was instrumental in securing a temporary financial assistance from the South Asia Regional Council of Ford Foundation. Finally, the author wishes to express his deepest appreciation to his wife, Nazma Khan, who was very patient and understanding during these trying years as a student wife and who has a marvelous job of typing this article.

Dr. Sazzad bin Shafique, Professor, Engineering at UTSA has been kind enough to redraw some of the drawing and suggest overall improvement.

REFERENCES

Bouharmont, J. 1962. Observations on somatic and meiotic chromosomes of <u>Oryza</u> species. Cytologia 27:258-275

Chao, L.F. 1928. Linkage studies in rice. Genetics 13:133-169

Chatterjee, D. 1951. Note on the origin and distribution of wild and cultivated rices. Indian J. Genet. Pl. Breed. 11(1):18-22

Darlington, C.D. 1937. Recent advances in cytology. Second Ed. Churchill Ltd. London. P.215

Henderson, M.T. 1964. Cytogenetic studies at the Louisiana Agricultural experiment station on the nature of intervarietal hybrid sterility on <u>Oryza</u> <u>sativa</u> L. Symp. Rice Genet. Cygenet., IRRI 1963 pp. 147-153. Elsevier Publishing co. , Amsterdam.

Henderson, M.T., B.P.Yeh and B.Exener. 1959. Further evidence of structural differentiation of chromosomes as a cause of sterility of intervarietal hybrids of rice, <u>Oryza sativa</u> L. Cytologia 24:415-422

Hu, C.H. 1958. Karyological studies in haploid plants. II. Analysis of karyotype and somatic pairing. Jap. J. Genet. 33;296-301 (in Japanese, English summary)

Hu, C.H. 1964. Further studies of meiosis in oryza species with special references to secondary association. Cytologia 27:285-295

Hu, C.H. 1964. Further studies in the chromosome morphology of <u>Oryza</u> <u>sativa</u> L. Symp. Rice Genet. Cytogenet. IRRI 1963 pp. 51-61. Elsevier Publishing Co., Amsterdam.

Ichijima, K. 1934. On the artificially induced mutations and polyploidy plants of rice occurring subsequent generations. Proc. Imp. (Japan) Acad. 10(6):388-391

Ishii, K., and S. Mitsukuri. 1960. Chromosome studies in <u>Oryza.</u> Somatic chromosomes of <u>Oryza</u> <u>sativa</u> L. Bull. Res. Coll. Agr. Vet. Med. Nion University 11:44-53

Jones, J. W., and A. E. Longley. 1941. Sterility and aberrant chromosome numbers in Caloro and other varieties of rice.   J. Agric. Res.(U.S.) 62:381-399

Khan, Sharafot H. 1975. A Technique for Staining Rice Chromosomes. Cytologia 40:595-598

Khan, Sharafot H., and S.H. Choudhury. 1965. (Unpublished M. Sc Ag. (thesis). Cytogenetical Studies on some rice varities (<u>Oryza</u> <u>sativa</u> L.) and their F1 hybrids. M.Sc. Ag thesis, East Pakistan (Bangladesh) Agricultural University.

Kuwada, Y. 1910. A cytological study of <u>Oryza</u> <u>sativa</u> L. Bot. Mag. 23:334-343

Lawrence, W. J.C. 1931. The secondary association of chromosomes. Cytologia 2: 352-384

McClintock, B. 1933. The association of non-homologous parts of chromosomes in the mid-prophase of meiosis in <u>Zea</u> mays. Z. Zell. Mikroskop. Abt. B. 19: 191-237

Mello-Sampayo, T. 1952. An inversion occurring in an F1 hybrid between two strains of <u>Oryza sativa</u> L. Genetica Iberica 4:43-45

Morinaga, T. 1964. Cytogenetical investigations on Oryza species. Symp. Rice Genet. Cytogenet. IRRI 1963. pp. 91-102. Elsevier publishing Co. , Amsterdam.

Morinaga, T. 1935. Cytogenetical studies on Oryza sativa L. II. Spontaneous autotriploid mutants in Oryza sativa L. Jap. J. Bot. 9:207-225

Morinaga, T., and E. Fukushima. 1934. Cytogenetical studies on Oryza sativa L. I. Studies on the haploid plant of Oryza sativa L. Jap. J. Bot. 7:73-106

Morishima, H., H. I. Oka and W.T. Chang. 1961. Directions of differentiations in populations of wild rice, Oryza sativa and Oryza sativa f. spontanea. Evolution 17:170-181

Nandi, H. K. 1936. The chromosome morphology, secondary association and origin of cultivated rice. J. Genet, 33:315-336

Oka, H.I. 1956. Phylogenetic differentiation in cultivated rice plant. 12. Polygenic nature of 'gametic development genes' controlling intervarietal hybrid sterility in rice. Jap. J. Breed. 6(1) : 51-55 (in Japanese, English summary)

Oka, H.I. 1957. Genic analysis for the sterility of hybrids between distantly related varieties of cultivated rice. J. Genet. 55:397-409

Parthasarathy, N. 1938. Cytological studies in Oryzeae and phalarideae. II. Further studies on Oryza . Cytologia 9:307-318

Pathak, G.N. 1940. Studies in the cytology of cereals. J. Genet, 39:437-467

Ramanujam, S. 1937. Cytogenetical studies in the Oryzeae. III. Cytogenetical behaviour of an interspecific hybrid in Oryza. J. Genet. 35:223-258

Ramiah, K. 1931. Preliminary investigations on the occurrence of an internpretation of non-homologous chromosome associations. Chromosomea (Berlin) 35:247-263

Ramiah, K. 1934. A haploid plant in rice. Indian Bot. Soc. Jour. 13:153-164

Ramiah, K., N. Parthasarathy and S. Ramanujam. 1933. Haploid plants in rice (Oryza sativa). Curr. Sci. 1:277-278

Richharia, R. H. 1960, Origin of cultivated rices. Indian J. Genet. Pl. Breed. 20:I-14

Riley, R., and V. Chapman. 1957. Haploids and polyhaploids in Aegilops and Triticum. Heredity 11:195-207

Riley, R., and V. Chapman. and C.N. Law. 1965.   Genetic variation in chromosome pairing. Adv. Genet. 13:57-107

Sadasivaiah, R.S., and K. J. Kasha. 1973. Non-homologous associations of haploid barley chromosomes in the cytoplasm of Hordeum bulbosum L. Canad J. Genet. Cytol. XV:45-52

Sadasivaih, R. S. and K.J. Kasha. 1971. Meiosis in haploid barely – mechanisms and speciation in Oryza. Symp. Rice Genet. Cytogenet. IRRI, 1963. Elsevier publishing Co., Amsterdam

Sakai, K. I. 1935. Chromosome studies in Oryza sativa L. I. The secondary association of meiotic chromosomes. Jap. J. Genet. II (3):145-156 (in Japanese, - quoted from Hu, 1962)

Sampath, S. 1962. The genus <u>Oryza</u>: its taxonomy and species interrelationships. Oryza 1:1-29

Sampath, S. and V. Krisnaswamy. 1948. A chromosome deficient paddy type. Curr. Sci. 17:271-272

Sears, E.R., and M. Okamoto. 1958. Intergenomic chromosome relationships in hexaploid wheat. Proc. Int. Cong. Genet. 10 (2) : 258-259

Selim, A. G. 1930. A cytological study of <u>Oryza sativa</u> L. Cytologia 2:1-26

Sen, S. K. 1963 Analysis of rice pachytene chromosomes. Nucleus 6(2) :107-120

Seshu, D.V., and T. Venkataswamy. 1958. A monosome in rice. Madras Agr. J. 45:311-314

Sethi, B. 1937. Cytological studies in paddy varities. Indian J. Agr. Sci. 7:687-706

Shastry, S.V.S. 1964. Chromosome structural differentiation, isolating sterility in rice <u>(Oryza</u> <u>sativa)</u>. Agr. And Livestock in India 1:414 - 426

Shastry, S.V.S., D.R. Ranga Rao and R.N. Misra. 1960. Pachytene analysis in <u>Oryza</u>. I. Chromosome morphology in <u>Oryza</u> <u>sativa</u>. Indian J. Genet. Pl. Breed. 20(1) : 15-21

Stebbins, G.L. 1956. Artificial polyploidy as a tool in plant breeding. Brookhaven Symp. Biol. 9: 37-52

Sybenga, J. 1966. The zygomere as a hypothetical unit of chromosome pairing initiation. Genetica 37 : 186-198

Sybenga, J. 1972. Chromosome-associated control of meiotic pairing differentiation. Variation within <u>Secale</u> <u>cereale.</u> Chromosoma 39:351-360

Sybenga, J. 1973. Allopolyploidization of autoploids. 2. Manipulation of the chromosome pairing system. Euphytica 22:433-444

Takahashi, H. 1936. On the rice plant raised the seeds produced by the haploid spikelets pollinated by the pollen of diploid plant. Proc. Soc. Agron. 8:355-363

Venlataswamy, 1957. Genetical and cytological studies of sterility in inter-racial hybrids of rice (Oryza sativa L.) Unpublished thesis, I.A.R.I., New Delhi.

Wu, H.k., S.C. Kwan and H.W. Li. 1964. A preliminary note on the pachytene analysis of <u>japonica</u> x <u>indica</u> hybrids. Symp. Rice Genet. Cytogenet. IRRI, 1963. Elsevier Publishing Co. , Amsterdam

Yao, S. Y., M.T. Henderson and N.E. Jadon. 1958. Cryptic structural hybridity as a probable cause of sterility in intervarietal hybrids of cultivated rice<u>, Oryza</u> <u>sativa</u> L. Cytologia 23:46-55

Yasui, K. 1941. Diploid bud formation in a haploid Oryza with some remarks on the behaviour of the nucleolus in mitosis. Cytologia 11:515-525

Yeh, B., and M. T. Henderson. 1961. Cytological studies in rice. Proc. Rice Tech. Work. Group (U.S.): MP-488:9-10

List of Tables

Table 1. Measurements of chromosomes in haploids (mitotic)

Chromosome	1	2	3	4	5	6	7	8	9	10	11	12
Cell												
1 length*	19.5	17.5	16.0	15.0	14.5	14.5	13.8	13.8	10.0	10.0	10.7	10.5
Arm ratio	.62	.89	.63	.36	.70	.70	.97	.97	.33	.33	.65	.69
2	22.0	18.0	17.0	15.5	14.5	14.5	12.5	12.5	11.0	11.0	7.0	7.0
	.67	.89	.67	.39	.45	.45	.92	.92	.83	.83	.67	.67
3	14.5	13.0	12.0	10.5	10.2	10.0	9.0	9.0	8.9	8.5	8.5	8.5
	.52	.86	.60	.40	.65	.67	.96	.96	.48	.54	.70	.70
4	15.5	13.5	13.0	12.0	11.5	11.5	10.5	10.5	10.2	10.2	9.4	9.4
	.52	.88	.63	.41	.77	.77	.84	.84	.45	.46	.70	.70
5	18.7	16.2	15.0	13.7	13.0	13.0	11.8	11.8	10.0	10.0	10.7	10.5
	.68	.85	.60	.33	.62	.62	.90	.90	.51	.51	.67	.67
6	17.1	14.9	14.0	12.9	12.3	12.3	11.2	11.2	10.0	10.0	9.0	9.0
	.63	.86	.58	.38	.50	.50	.89	.89	.36	.42	.63	.63
7	16.6	14.6	13.5	12.1	11.6	11.5	10.4	10.4	9.4	9.3	8.6	8.6
	.62	.88	.58	.40	.63	.60	.97	.97	.46	.46	.65	.65
8	15.0	13.2	12.5	11.3	10.3	10.3	9.7	9.7	9.5	9.5	10.7	10.5
	.56	.89	.63	.42	.58	.58	.92	.92	.33	.38	.65	.65
9	18.8	16.5	14.5	13.5	13.0	13.0	12.6	12.5	10.1	10.1	10.0	10.0
	.67	.87	.60	.35	.67	.67	.88	.88	.45	.45	.69	.69
10	17.0	15.3	14.0	12.8	12.3	12.2	11.4	11.4	9.9	9.9	9.2	9.2
	.70	.89	.61	.36	.65	.65	.96	.96	.38	.38	.71	.71
Average Length	17.5	15.3	14.2	12.9	12.3	12.3	11.3	11.3	9.9	9.9	9.0	9.0
Average Arm Ratio	.62	.88	.61	.38	.62	.62	.92	.92	.46	.48	.67	.67
Percent of Chromatin length	12.08	10.56	9.80	8.90	8.49	8.49	7.80	7.80	6.83	6.83	6.21	6.21

*length measurements are in millimeters from Camera Lucida drawings at a magnification of approximately 6000x.

Table 2. Mean length and range in microns, arm ratios, percentage of total chromatin lengths for the 12 chromosomes of rice, <u>O.</u> <u>sativa</u> L., at mitotic metaphase of haploids.

Chromosome	1	2	3	4	5	6	7	8	9	10	11	12	Total
mean length in microns	2.90	2.55	2.37	2.15	2.05	2.05	1.88	1.88	1.65	1.65	1.50	1.50	24.13
range in microns	2.4 to 3.6	2.17 to 3.00	2.00 to 2.83	2.00 to 2.58	1.70 to 2.42	1.70 to 2.42	1.50 to 2.30	1.50 to 2.30	1.57 to 1.83	1.57 to 1.83	1.17 to 1.78	1.17 to 1.78	
arm ratio	0.62	0.88	0.61	0.38	0.62	0.62	0.92	0.92	0.46	0.48	0.67	0.67	
percentage of total chromatin length	12.08	10.56	9.80	8.90	8.49	8.49	7.80	7.80	6.83	6.83	6.21	6.21	100.00

Table 3.   Comparison of the data obtained by the different investigators regarding
Chromosome lengths and position of centromere

	Yasui (1941) RT;length hapl. class: % of total	HU (1958) RT; length hapl.class: % of total	Ishii Mitsukori (1960) RT; length hapl. class % of total	Idem (1964) RT; length dipl. class % of total	HU (1960) RT; length hapl. class % of total	Shastry et al. (1960) pmc. length dipl. class % of total	Khan, S.H. (present study) RT. lenght hapl .class % of total-
1	5.0 SM 12.3	2.4 SM 11.5	4.2 SM 12.2	3.5 SM 12.0	4.3 SM 13.0	79.0 SM 19.7	2.9 SM 12.08
2	4.5 M 11.0	2.2 ST 10.6	3.9 M 11.3	3.2 SM 11.0	3.7 SM 11.1	47.5 SM 11.9	2.55 SM 10.96
3	4.1 M 10.6	2.2 M 10.6	3.4 SM 9.8	2.9 SM 10.0	3.3 M 9.8	47.0 M 11.8	2.37 SM 9.8
4	3.8 M 9.4	1.9 M 9.0	3.2 ST* 9.3	2.6 ST 8.90	2.9 M 8.7	38.5 SM* 9.6	2.15 ST 8.9
5	3.7 SM 9.1	1.7 SM 8.2	3.1 SM 9.1	2.4 SM* 8.3	2.9 SM 8.6	30.5 SM 7.6	2.05 SM 8.49
6	3.5 SM 8.6	1.6 SM 7.7	2.8 M 8.1	2.4 SM 8.3	2.8 ST 8.3	27.5 ST 6.9	2.05 SM 8.49
7	3.1 SM 7.6	1.6 ST* 7.7	2.7 ST 7.8	2.3 SM 7.9	2.6 SM 7.8	26.5 M 6.6	1.88 SM 7.8
8	3.0 SM 7.4	1.6 ST* 7.7	2.5 SM 7.2	2.2 SM 7.2	2.6 SM* 7.8	23.0 SM 5.8	1.88 SM 7.8
9	2.9 M 7.1	1.5 SM 7.2	2.4 SM 7.0	2.0 SM 6.9	2.3 SM 6.8	21.0 SM 5.2	1.65 ST*/SM 6.83
10	2.6 ST* 6.4	1.5 M 7.2	2.3 SM 6.7	2.0 SM 6.9	2.3 M 6.7	21.0 ST 5.2	1.65 ST*/SM 6.83
11	2.3 SM 5.7	1.4 M 6.7	2.1 M 6.1	1.9 SM 6.6	2.0 ST* 6.0	20.5 SM 5.1	1.5 SM 6.21
12	2.0 SM 4.9	1.2 SM 5.8	1.9 SM 5.5	1.6 M 5.5	1.8 SM 5.4	18.0 SM 4.5	1.5 SM 6.21
100/	40.00	20.80	34.50	29.00	33.50	400.00	24.13

RT = Root Tip   * = nucleolar   dipl.= diploid   SM= Submedian   xCa=measure   ST=Subterminal
PMC=Pollen Mother Cell   chromosome   hapl.= haploid   M = Median   (/u) =Micron   centromere

List of Figures

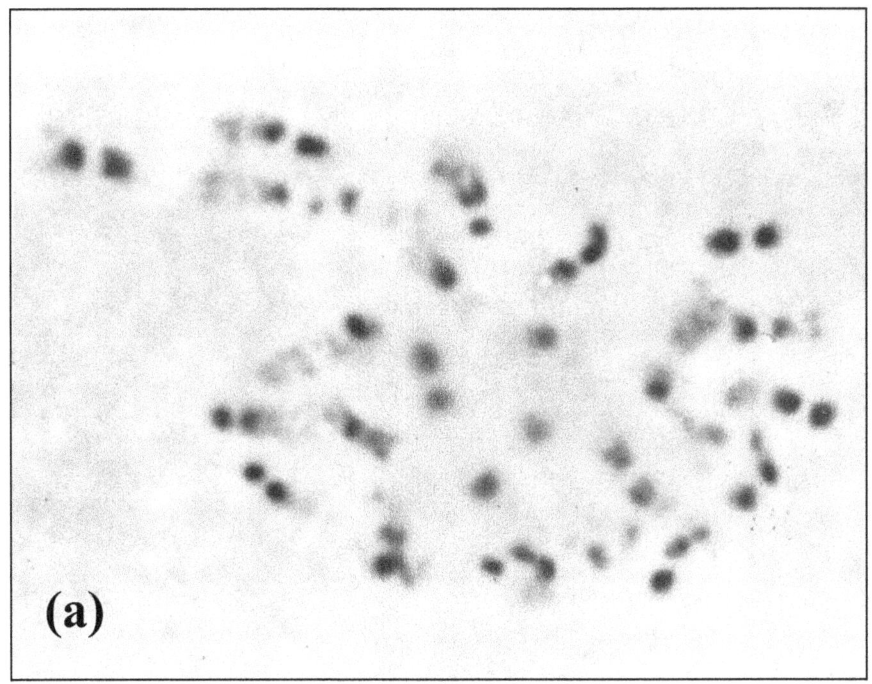

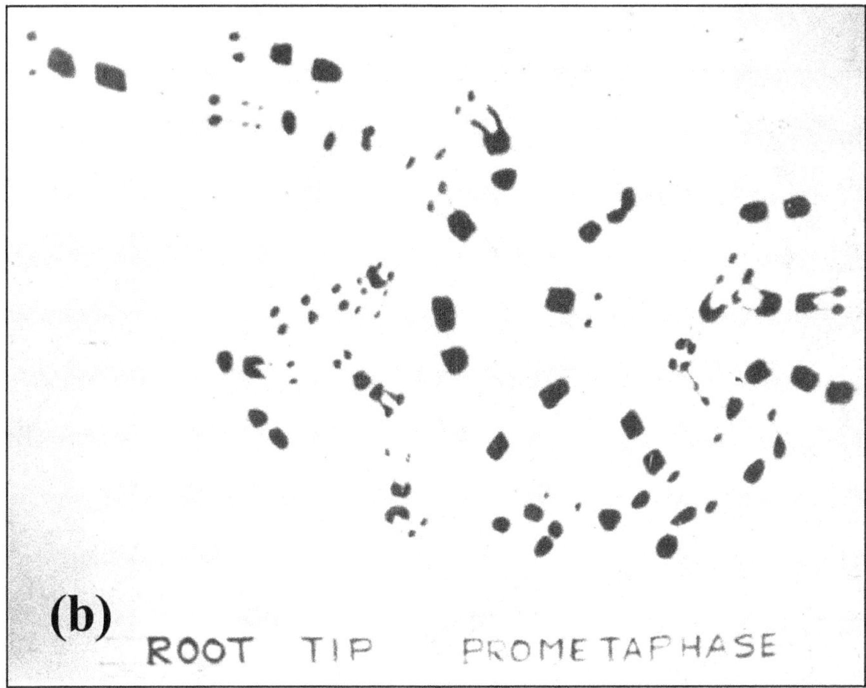

Fig. 1: Root Tip Prometaphase of: (a) Calrose showing secondary constrictions in most of the chromosomes and (b) Camera Lucida drawing of the above cell.

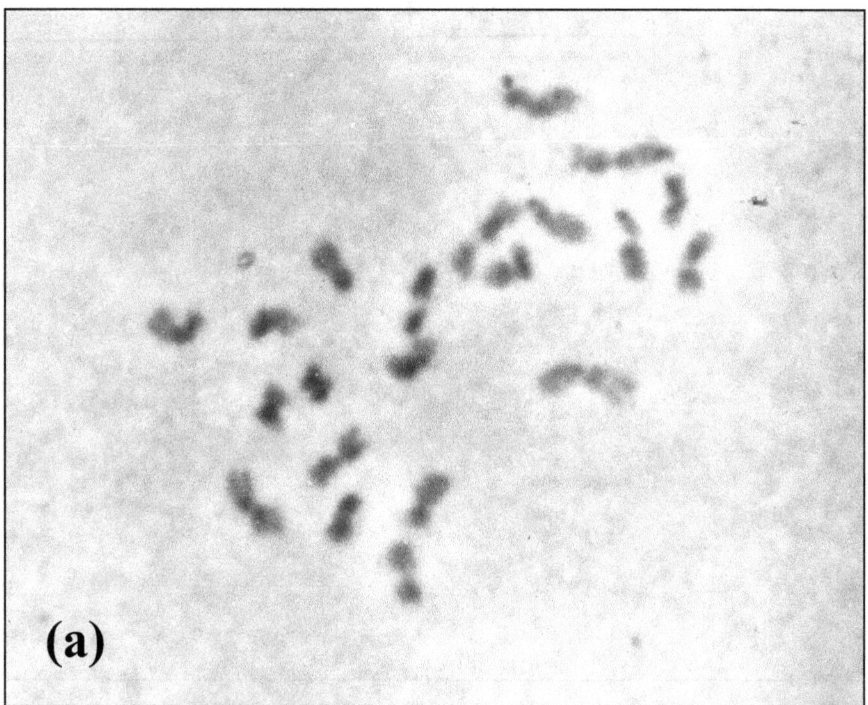

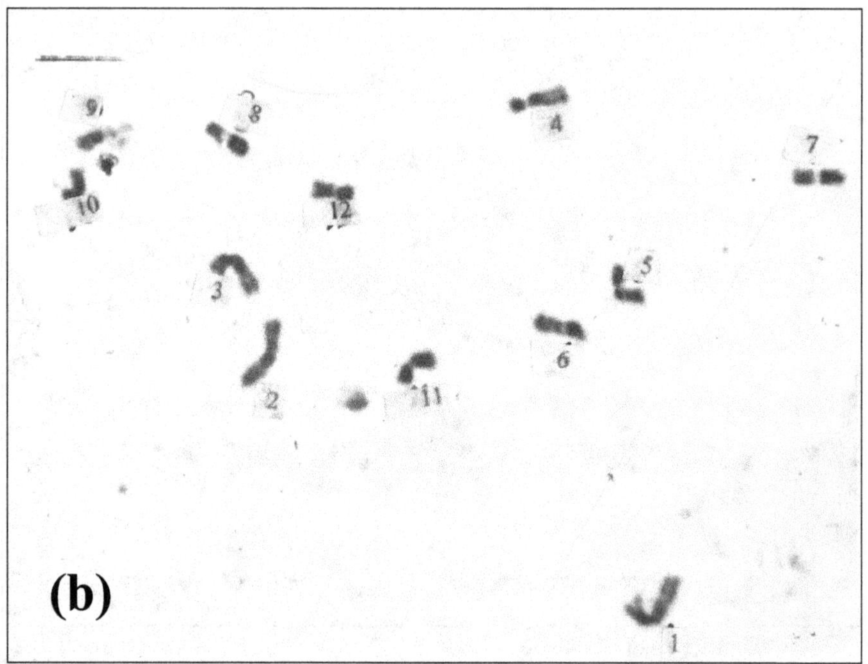

Fig. 2: Root Tip Metaphase of: (a) CS-M3 showing secondary constriction in six pairs of chromosomes and (b) CS-M3 haploids showing centromeric and other secondary constriction.

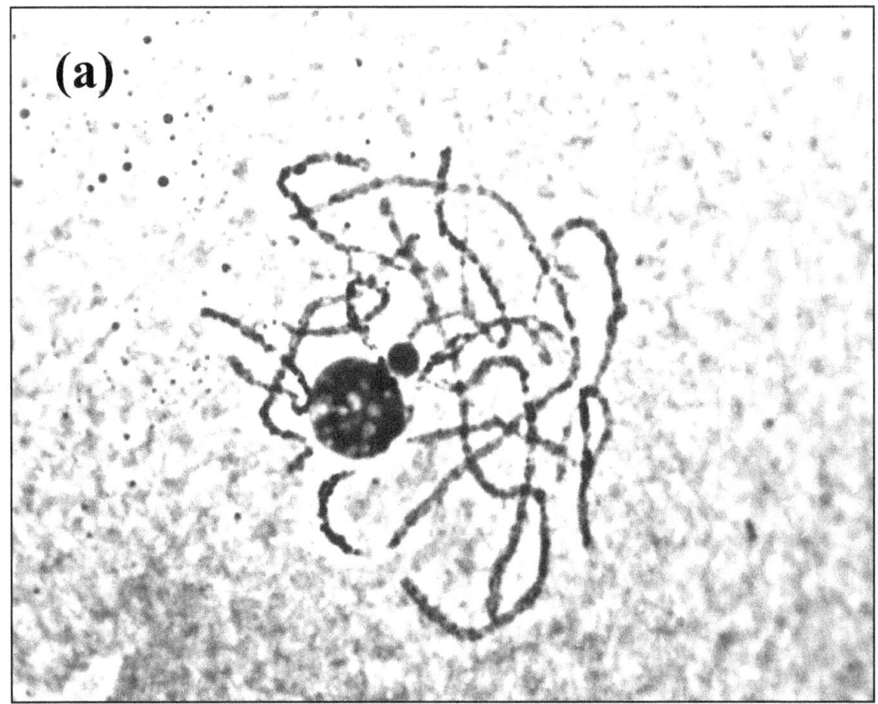

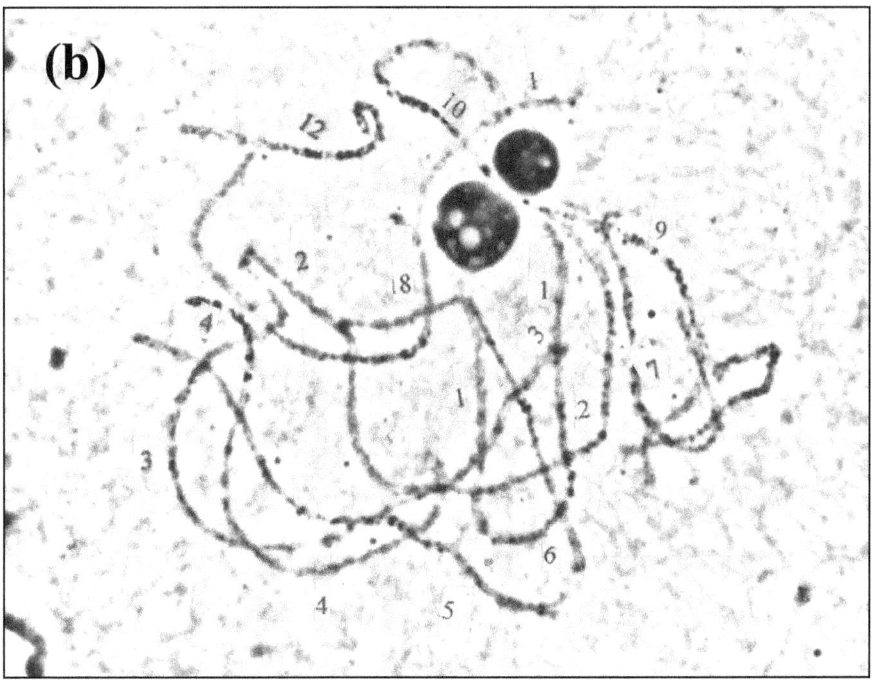

Fig. 3: Pachytene in PMC of CS-M3: (a) Several chromosomes are seen attached to the main nuleolus and (b) Showing the bivalents streched out resolving into smaller chromemeres whereas some chromosomes retained their chromomeric patteren.

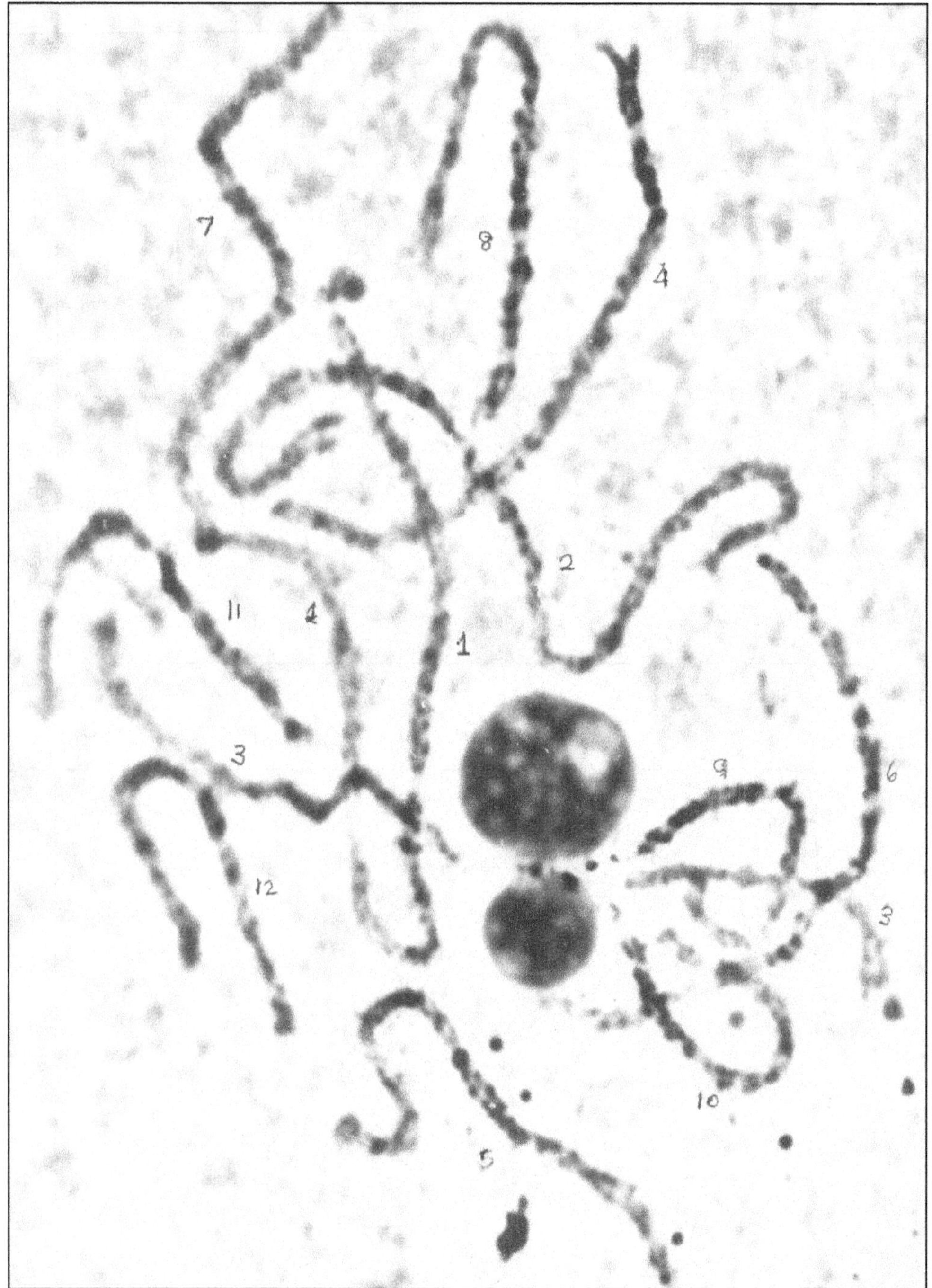

Fig. 4: Pachytene in CS-M3 showing characteristic chromeric patterns for most chromosomes. Similarities in chromemeric patterns and general appearance is evident for chromosomes 5, 6; 7, 8; 9, 10; and 11, 12.

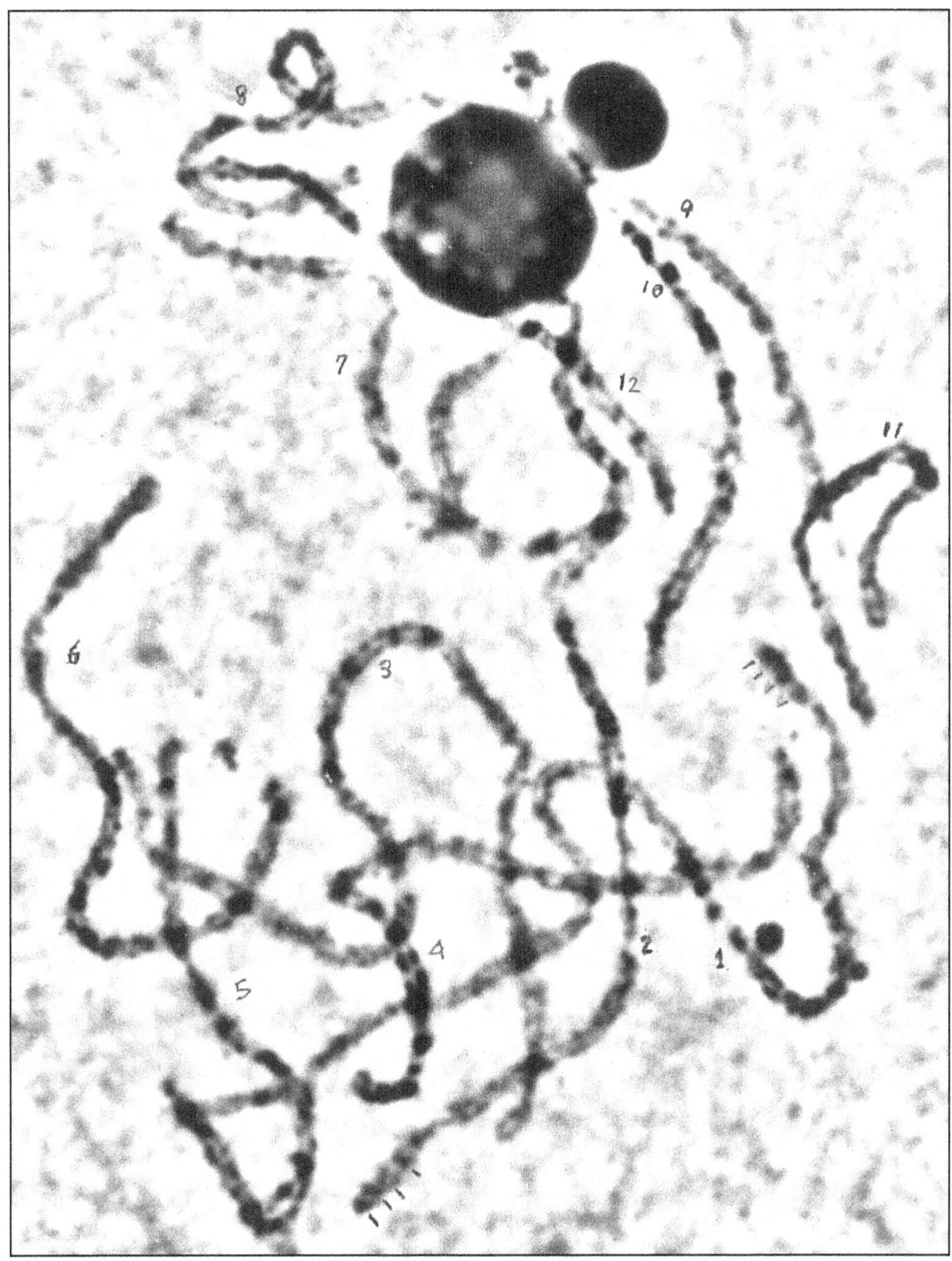

Fig. 5: Pachytene in CS-M3 showing chromosomes 1 and 2 having similar distal ends. (indicated by arrows)

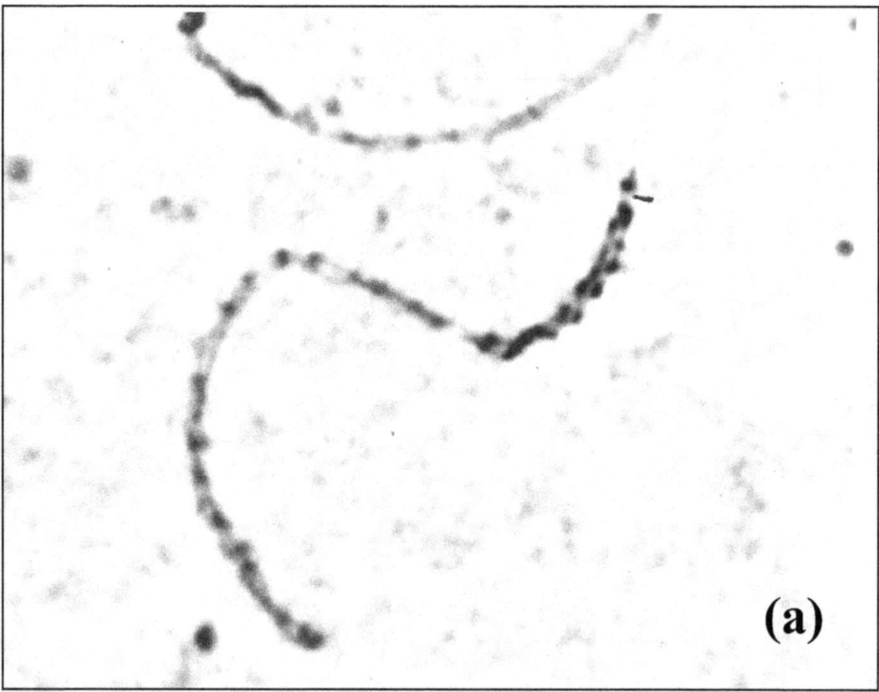

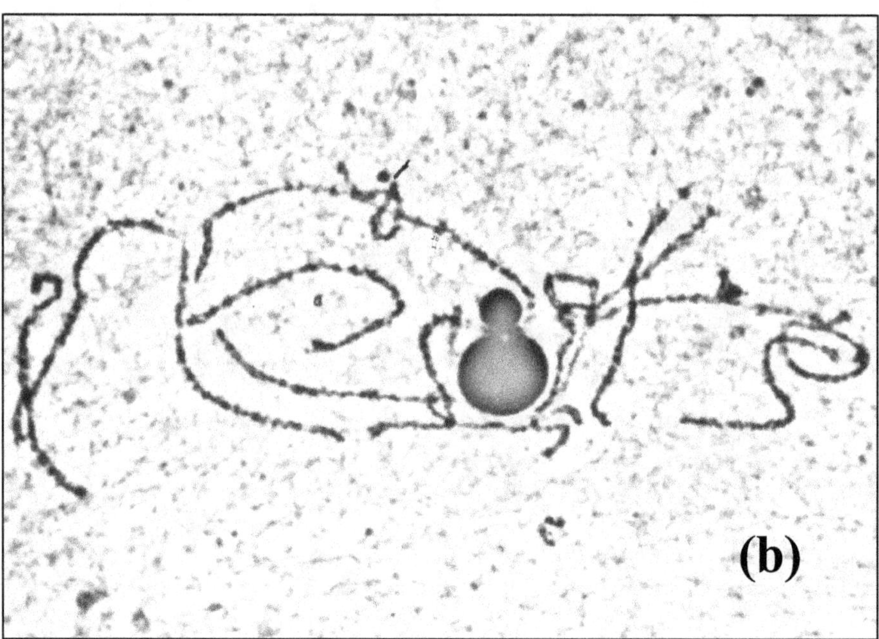

Fig. 6:   Chromosome 4 of Pachytene in CS-M3: (a) the satellitic gap on the short arm of chromosome and (b) small nuleolar body produced at he end of the chromosome. (indicated by arrows)

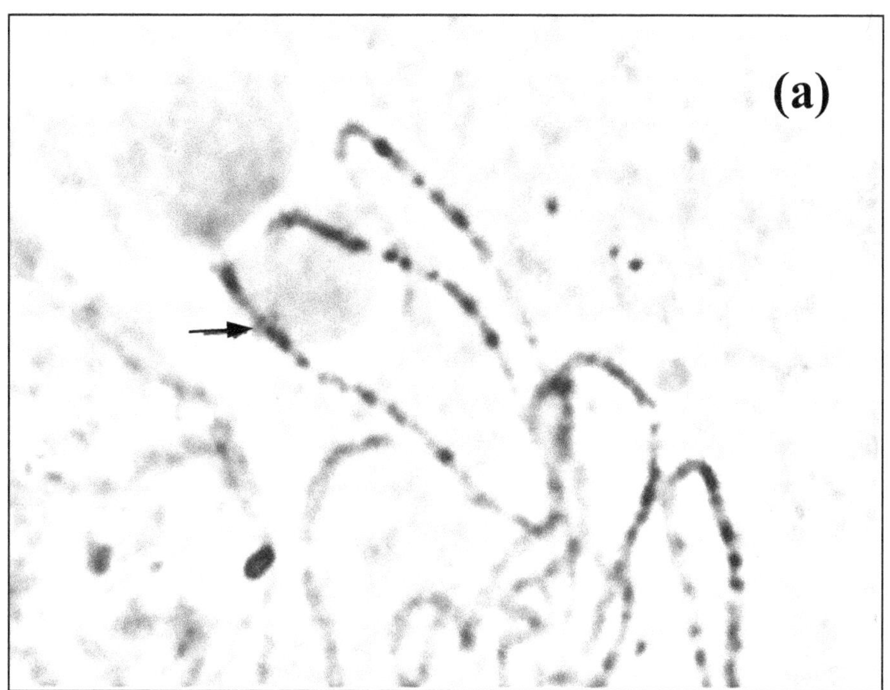
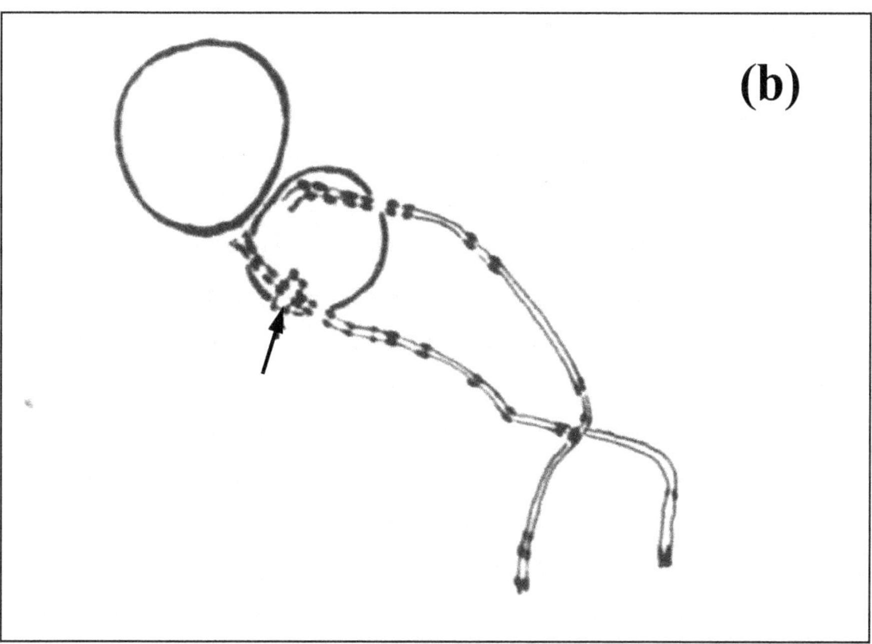

Fig. 7:   T(N)-1 Pachytene: (a) the 'collar' configuration on the short arm of chromosome 9 and (b) Camera Lucida drawing of the 'collar' configuration. (indicated by arrows)

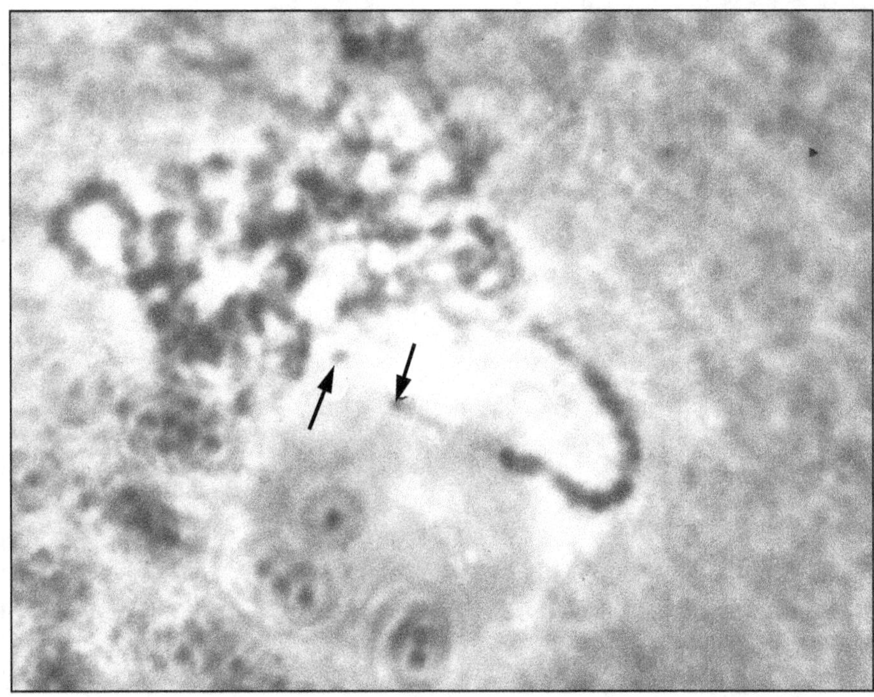

Fig. 8:   Pachytene in haploid CS-M3-2. Arrow indicates chromosome 9 and 10 paired.

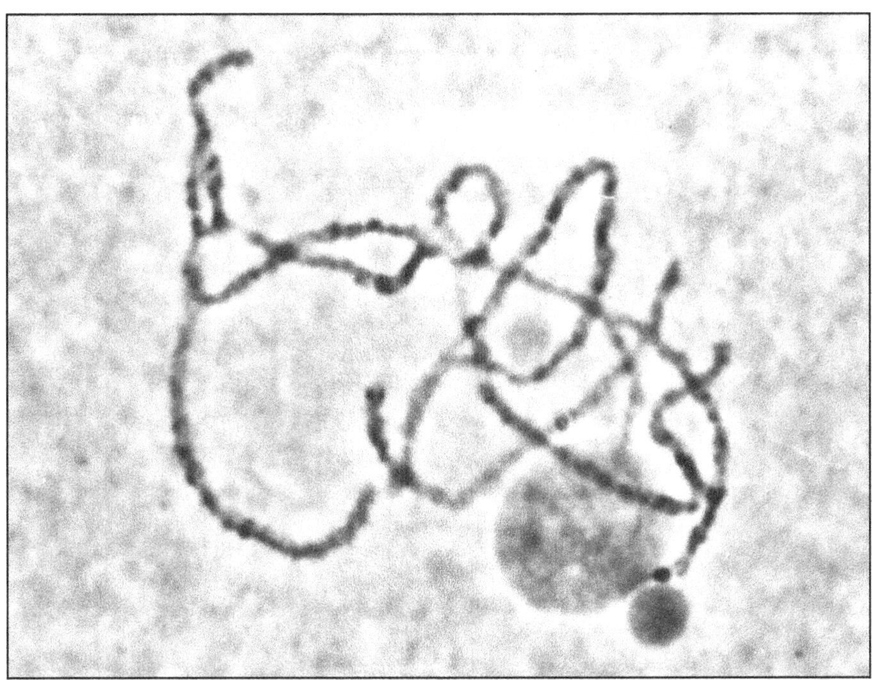

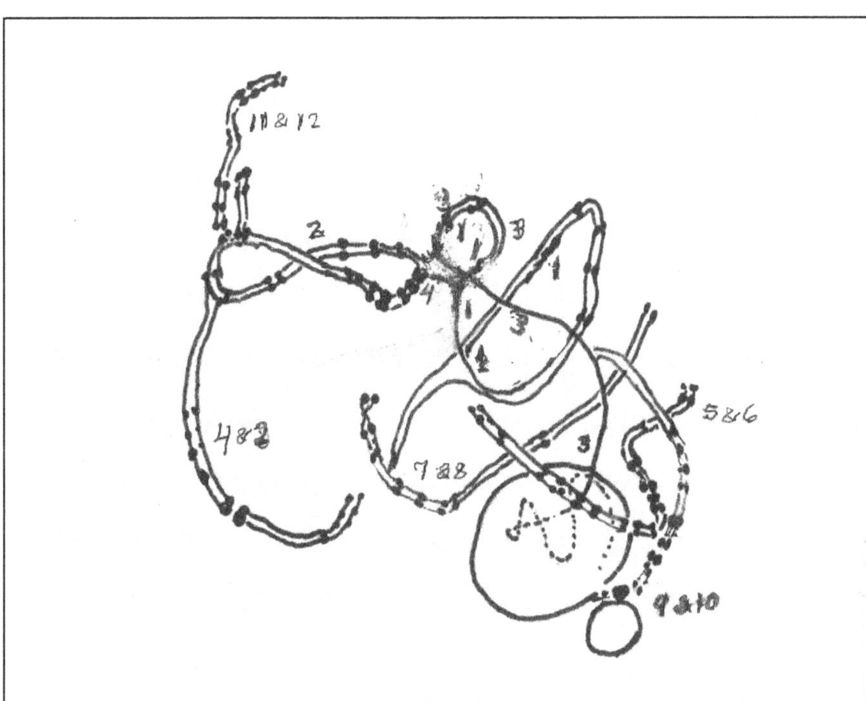

Fig. 9: Pachytene in haploid CS-M3: (a) showing complete pairing between the chromosomes. Arrow indicates the multivalent involving the four largest chromosomes and (b) Camera Lucida drawing of the completely paired chromosomes.

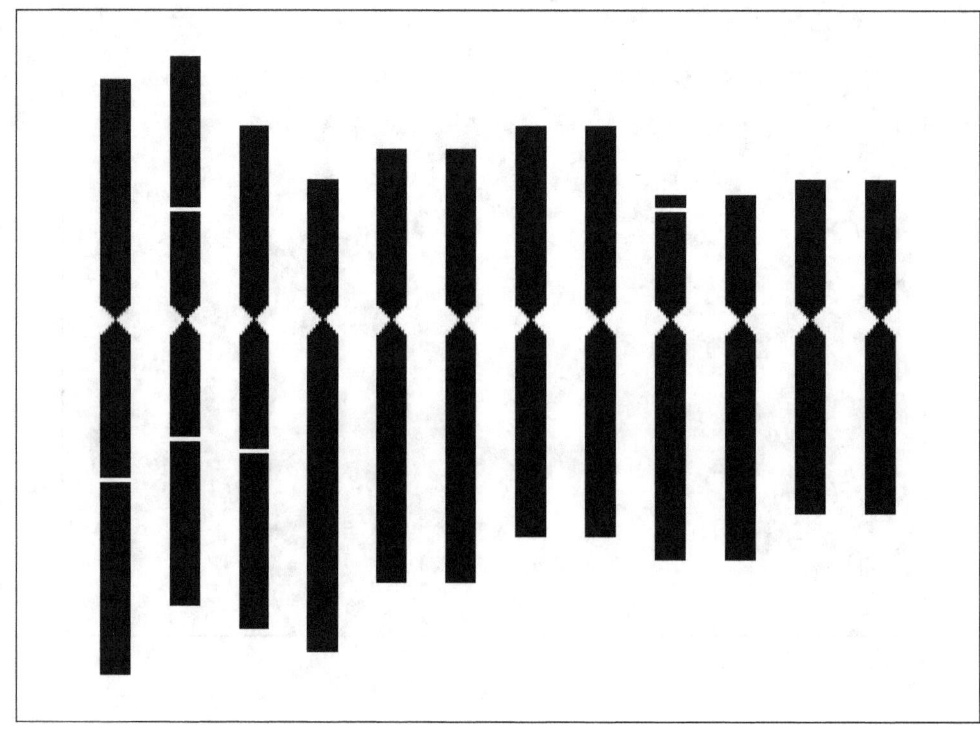

Fig. 10: Idiogram showing the revised karyotype of rice, <u>Oryza</u> <u>sativa</u> L.

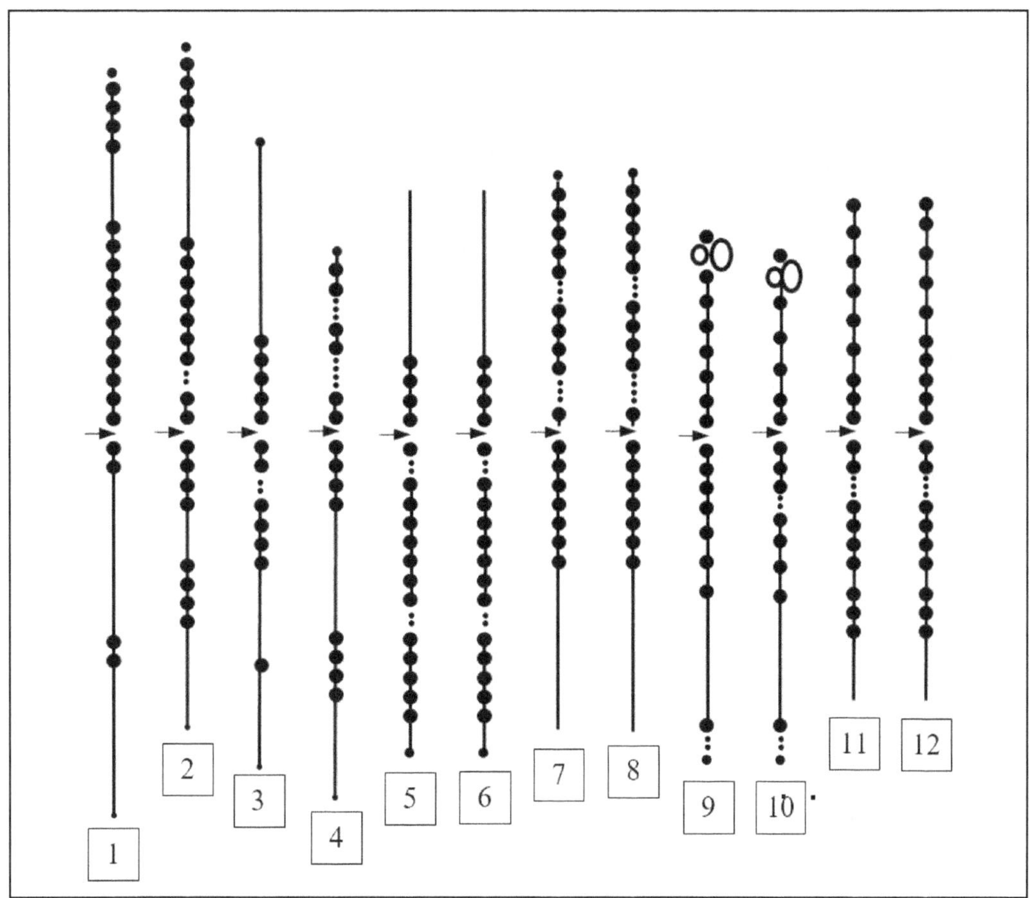

Fig. 11: Chrometric patterns for the 12 chromosomes of rice, _Oryza_ _sativa_ L.

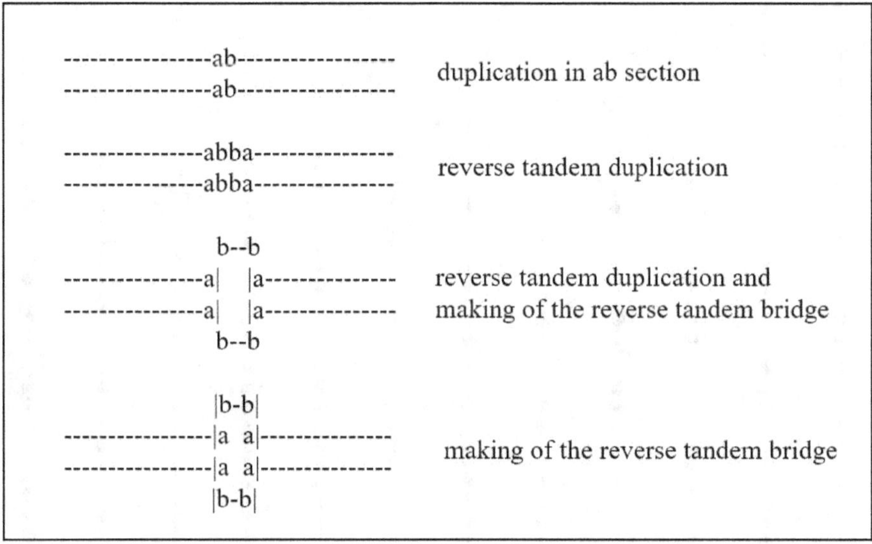

Fig. 12:   Diagrammatic illustration of the 'Collar' configuration on the short arm of Chromosome 9.

Fig. 13: Diagrammatic illustration of the origin of rice.

<pre>
2 ------oooo c oo-ooooo-----oooo   2 ------oooo c oo-ooooo-----oooo

2'------oooo c oo-oooo|o-----oooo   2'/ 4 -----oooo c oo-oooo-o

                Break point

3' ------oooo c oooo----|o   3'/1 --------oooo c oooo----oooo-----oooo

3 ------oooo c oooo----o   3 --------oooo c oooo-----o
</pre>

Fig. 14: Translocation the two marked chromosomes for 1, 2, 3, and 4 pairing in diploids –
original vs. modified chromosomes.